Work Experience:

Expanding opportunities for undergraduates

Lee Harvey, Vicki Geall and Sue Moon

**with Jane Aston, Lindsey Bowes
and Alison Blackwell**

Centre
for
Research
into
Quality

Work Experience: Expanding opportunities for undergraduates

Lee Harvey, Vicki Geall and Sue Moon
with Jane Aston, Lindsey Bowes and Alison Blackwell

© Lee Harvey, Vicki Geall and Sue Moon, 1998

Centre for Research into Quality,
The University of Central England in Birmingham,
90 Aldridge Road, Perry Barr, Birmingham, B42 2TP

Project Administrator: Lesley Plimmer

British Library Cataloguing-in-Publication Data
A catalogue record for this book is available from the British Library
ISBN 1-85920 113 X

UNIVERSITY COLLEGE

MEMORANDUM

TO: Meryl Bradshaw
           Andrea Harper

FROM: Phill Lloyd

DATE: 22 May 1998

REF: PL/KMB/383

I have attached copies of the Work Experience: Expanding opportunities for undergraduates. Can we arrange to meet at some time before the end of term to discuss the implications of this booklet. Can you please liaise with Karen to fix up a mutually convenient time.

Contents

Acknowledgements

We are indebted to the people who gave up their time to participate in the research. We also want to take this opportunity to thank all the people in the organisations who helped us to arrange interviews.

We have had invaluable support from the Project Steering Committee at all stages of this research: Richard Brown, Council for Industry in Education (CIHE), Margaret Wallis, Association of Graduate Careers Advisory Service (AGCAS), Roly Cockman, Association of Graduate Recruiters (AGR), David Pierce, Department for Education and Employment (DfEE), Malcolm Brewer, Association of Sandwich Education and Training (ASET), Jenny Naish, National Centre for Work-Based Learning Partnerships (NCWBLP), Liz Rhodes, Shell Technology Enterprise Programme (STEP), Richard Barron, Marks and Spencer and Jane Groves, British Steel.

The Council for Industry and Higher Education (CIHE), established some ten years ago, is an informal, entirely independent group of company chairs or people of similar standing, and heads of Universities and Colleges. It aims to encourage industry and higher education to work together and represent joint thinking to government. Its discussions enable companies to make better informed judgements about what their own activities and relationships might best be with Universities and Colleges and help vice-chancellors and principals to understand industry's perceptions and interest.

The Centre for Research into Quality (CRQ) is based at the University of Central England in Birmingham (UCE) and was established to provide independent, high-quality research services in the higher education sector. CRQ specialises in research and evaluation of higher education policy at a sector and institutional level. CRQ is one of the leading higher education research institutes in Britain and has an international reputation for its work, with frequent requests to participate in national and international forums. The Centre has undertaken consultancy in Europe, Africa, Australasia, South-East Asia and the Americas. Over the last decade, CRQ's eight-strong team has developed expertise in most areas of higher education, especially quality, the higher-education employer interface, funding and learning and teaching.

This work was produced under contract with the Department for Education and Employment. The views expressed are those of the authors and do not necessarily reflect those of the Department for Education and Employment or any other Government Department.

1 Context

Work experience in higher education is not a new concept. Indeed, professional practice in relation to the clergy, medicine and law formed the foundations for higher education, and throughout its history there has been a recognition of work experience in term of its benefits for students, employers and the nation's economic success.

More recently, in 1955, industrial placements were advocated for engineering and technology courses by the National Council for Technological Awards. The emphasis on vocationalism in the Robbins Report (GBCHE, 1963) led to the development of polytechnics in the 1960s and the significant development of sandwich courses.

The Enterprise in Higher Education initiative, established in 1987, aimed to have a direct impact on higher education courses. It was, in part, a response to the needs of an expanding higher education sector itself becoming more responsive to labour market demands. Its focus was on the development of the 'employability' skills of undergraduates. Courses in the United Kingdom (UK) would have to be broader, more flexible and give deliberate prominence to what were coming to be called 'transferable and intellectual personal skills' (Wright, 1992).

In addition, the Department for Education and Employment has been funding a wide range of development projects aimed at helping higher education become more relevant, responsive and flexible to the needs of employers and the economy. They have established over 40 projects in the last decade and a significant number have been concerned with work-based learning. Three series of projects have been supported (1990–92, 1992–94, 1996–98). They have been mainly concerned with raising the status and practice of learning at and through work and integrating it with more traditional forms of learning. In particular they have explored how it might be stimulated and exposed and given value through some sort of accreditation (Brennan and Little, 1996).

Work experience has re-emerged as a significant issue in higher education and the research reported here attempts to identify strategies to increase work-experience opportunities and to ensure that these opportunities offer a meaningful experience – that they are learning opportunities. There is a difference, therefore, between 'working' and undertaking a period of work experience. 'Work experience' is defined as a period of work that is designed to encourage reflection on the experience and to identify the learning that comes from working.

Why is work experience a crucial issue now?

The current emphasis on work experience is symptomatic of the ever-more rapidly changing world of work. Work experience is increasingly sought by employers during recruitment and a range of relevant experiences will better equip graduates for the flexible workplace of the future.

Public and private sector organisations have been forced to change in response to a number of factors. Financial pressures, global competition, a focus on core value added, the impact of information technology and an ever-increasing emphasis on meeting rising customer expectations have changed the nature of many organisations (Harvey, Moon and Geall, 1997). Changes within organisations, such as 'downsizing', 'delayering' and the move to more flexible contractual arrangements, all have an impact on the careers and requisite attributes of graduate employees.

Large organisations that have a tradition of recruiting graduates, may no longer be offering traditional, graduate-training schemes and, increasingly, graduates are being employed in small and medium enterprises (SMEs) with no initial training schemes. The result is increasing pressure on graduates to be immediately effective in a range of roles (NCIHE, 1997).

The future changing nature of work requires graduates to be 'work-ready' following graduation to ensure economic competitiveness in a global context. Not only is there an expectation that graduates should be immediately effective but also that they should be able to help the organisation deal with, and ultimately lead, change.

Graduates are having to fulfil these roles in changing organisations. An important focus is their need to develop as lifelong learners to become effective members of learning organisations (see Chapter 2 for discussion).

Work experience has an important role to play in the development of work readiness but also in the development of students as lifelong learners. There is increasing emphasis being placed on lifelong learning, which suggests that learning is something that goes on in the workplace as well as the academy. This raises the profile of work experience, not just as a work-readiness opportunity, but as a means to aiding the process of learning through work. Thus work experience as part of the undergraduate experience can, for example, be seen as a precursor to, and facilitator of, continuing professional development.

There have been a number of major reviews of work experience (RISE, 1985; Davies 1990; Brennan and Little, 1996), and government funding initiatives (such as Enterprise in Higher Education) aimed at encouraging the development of work experience opportunities (TIHR, 1990; EDG, 1991; Elton, 1993; HMI, 1993).

Previous research (Banta, *et al.*, 1991; Hansen, 1991; Harvey with Green, 1994) has identified the importance of work experience as a major factor in developing work readiness. Indeed, work experience is a 'missing ingredient' in undergraduate education, at least from the perspective of employers. *Graduates' Work* (Harvey, Moon and Geall, 1997, p. 2) concludes that:

> If there was to be a single recommendation to come from the research, it would be to encourage all undergraduate programmes to offer students an option of a year-long work placement and employers to be less reluctant to provide placement opportunities.

The National Committee of Inquiry into Higher Education (NCIHE), drawing on *Graduates' Work*, also placed considerable emphasis on work experience in its final report, concluding *inter alia* that 'students can benefit from experience in many different settings, structured and informal, paid and unpaid. Their academic experience should help them understand how experience relates to their personal and future development' (NCIHE, 1997, para. 9.30). Three principal recommendations about expanding opportunities for students to undertake work experience, to develop employability skills and improving links between higher education and employers, were made in the Report, one aimed at institutions, one at government and the other at companies:

> We recommend that all institutions should, over the medium term, identify opportunities to increase the extent to which programmes help students to become familiar with work, and help them to reflect on such experience.
>
> (Recommendation 18)

> We recommend that the Government, with immediate effect, works with representative employer and professional organisations to encourage employers to offer more work experience opportunities for students.
>
> (Recommendation 19)

> We recommend that companies should take a strategic view of their relationship with higher education and apply the same level of planning to it that they give to other aspects of their operations.
>
> (Recommendation 30)

Aims and Objectives of the Work Experience Project

The research reported here explores what can be done to increase the opportunities for undergraduates to gain work experience and how the learning from these experiences can be maximised. The project has aimed to specify the range and variety of work experience for undergraduates.

In suggesting ways of increasing the quantity, quality and relevance of work experience in its various forms the research has attempted to identify the constraints to such expansion and how they might best be reduced or removed. The study outlines what can be learned from models of best practice and suggests a range of options that employers can use.

The research addresses these issues by:

- providing a definitive mapping of the range and variety of work experience;

- providing an account of the organisational issues related to establishing and accrediting each type of work experience;

- exploring and assessing the value of the different types of work experience from the point of view of:
  - employers;
  - undergraduate students and recent graduates;
  - teachers in higher education;

- identifying ways in which to encourage employers to offer more work experience to students;

- outlining ways in which higher education institutions could develop the opportunities for students to undertake work experience;

- specifying the constraints on further expansion of provision and recognition of work-experience opportunities for each type of work experience.

The research explores possibilities within a range of different models of work-based learning (Brennan and Little, 1996; Wallis, 1997) with a focus on both public and private sectors, large and small organisations. The practical focus of the research is complemented by an analysis of how different types of work experience reflect different approaches to organisational flexibility, drawing on the model of the workplace profile developed in *Graduates' Work*.

Multiple perspectives

What distinguishes learning through work experience from much other learning in higher education is the partnerships between the range of stakeholders who are involved. The research considers the expansion of the quantity, and enhancement of the quality, of work experience from the point of view of the key parties. In most instances this involves at least two, but more often three or four parties: students, employers, academic teaching staff, higher education institutional management, broker agencies, or professional bodies. If there is to be an increase in the quantity and quality of work experience opportunities then there needs to be:

- a recognition of the parties involved;

- clear links between the parties;

- a clarification of how each stakeholder group might benefit in both the immediate and the long term.

> A placement is a partnership between the university, the employer and the student. If any one of the three don't fulfil their obligations, then 'it's all off'. (Morley, 1997)

It is, therefore, necessary to examine the objectives and effectiveness of work experience from these different perspectives to establish what is working and what can be expanded. In particular, the research focused on:

1. *Students* as lifelong learners.

2. *Employers* as having both immediate economic imperatives and as employers of lifelong learners, both necessary for the future of the organisation.

3. *Teachers* as having a subject focus and as facilitators of lifelong learning.

4. *'Brokers'* as having a bridging or supervising role and increasingly assessing the work experience element in relation to both the programme of study and lifelong learning.

Methodology

The research process involved the following stages:

- an exploratory-descriptive stage identifying current practice and terminology;

- an analytic stage exploring examples of work-based learning in practice and examining how it develops the skills and knowledge of students;

- a critical-reflective stage exploring stakeholder views of the role of work-based learning and devising an approach to assess the impact of work-based learning at a personal, organisational and system level.

The project has employed a number of methods in consulting widely with people who are involved in the wide range of work experience (Appendix 3). These have included visits, telephone interviews and literature reviews to establish a picture of a vast range of work experience initiatives currently being undertaken. Initiatives explored include:

- programme-, department- or faculty-specific initiatives;

- institution-wide initiatives;

- student employment bureaux;

- initiatives between Training Enterprise Councils (TECs) and higher education institutions;

- initiatives between TECs and other local or regional organisations;

- employer organisation initiatives (for example, ASDA, Tesco, Guinness);

- work-experience brokers (for example, Shell STEP, Business Bridge);

- student associations (for example, Student Industrial Society (SIS), L'Association Internationale des Étudiants en Sciences et Commerciales (AIESEC));

- national voluntary agencies (for example, GAP, Youth for Britain, Year in Industry).

The research draws on the large body of knowledge about work-experience and work-related learning that already exists, using published books and papers on issues related to work-based learning and competencies in higher education, and relevant contributions from industry and commerce. The research has also drawn on the considerable experience of the Project Steering Group (see Acknowledgements).

There has been a re-analysis of empirical data already collected by the Centre for Research into Quality (CRQ), and the reflections of students on their STEP placements. Anonymous quotes attributed to employers and recent graduates derive from interviews undertaken as part of the field work for *Graduates' Work*. There has also been the collection of some new empirical data from students through a CRQ questionnaire asking sandwich placement students about their work experience.

Types of work experience

Work experience for undergraduates takes a wide variety of forms. Most of these are opportunities taken by full-time undergraduates as many part-timers are already working while they study. Some part-time students use their paid work as reflective 'work experience opportunities' (as opposed to just experience of work) and others also avail themselves of new 'work experience opportunities' to widen their experience.[1] The discussion of work experience should, thus, not just be seen to refer to young, full-time students. Indeed, the report suggests that work experience is relevant for:

---

1   Part-time students in full-time work have an experience of work but rarely reflect on the skills and abilities they have developed and often do not link their undergraduate subject to their workplace setting. Sometimes this overt reflection does occur. Students do not stop learning outside the academic setting. However, the extent to which the full- or part-time work undertaken by part-time students is indicative of 'a work-experience opportunity' is dependent on whether or not the learning from such settings is 'captured'. This is discussed further below and in Chapter 2.

- traditional school leavers;
- full-time, mature students who may have had experience of work but not reflected on it;
- part-time students in work who may need some guidance on reflection and evaluation of work experience in order to add value;
- part-time unemployed students.

There are work experiences for undergraduates embedded in the programme of study and experiences gained from extra-curricular activities. Some extra-curricular work experiences are organised with educational or career-development objectives in mind. Other forms of work experience mainly result from the needs of students who pursue specific interests (on a voluntary basis) or to earn money. (See Appendix 1 for extended details of the varieties of work experience).

Part of the programme of study

Work experience, as part of the programme of study, takes four broad forms:

- placing students in a supervised work setting for a specified number of weeks as part of a sandwich course (usually for an academic or calendar year) or to provide a number of periods of professional experience in disciplines where there is a professional or regulatory body requirement that students undertake practical work as part of the undergraduate study;
- providing students with the opportunity to undertake short periods of work experience, usually relevant to their discipline;
- arranging for students to undertake employer-linked project work, either on an individual or team basis;
- arranging work-place visits, or case study simulations, to give students a brief insight into a particular world of work.

Within each of these there are considerable variations in the procedures. However, it is possible to identify the main objectives, typical length and extent of student participation (Figure 1.1).

Figure 1.1   Undergraduate work experience (and experience relevant to work) as part of a programme of study (Appendix 1)

	Type	Typical length (weeks)	Objectives (for student)	Student participation
1	Sandwich course	40–48	Structured immersion in 'relevant' work setting	Many (50,000)
2	Professional experience	20–40*	To develop competence to practice	Many
3	Work-experience element	2–15	Opportunity for development in 'real' work setting	Some, increasing
4	Overseas placement	12–26	Widen experience, develop employability skills and language competence	Some (c. 1500)
5	Work-linked individual project	1–26	Problem solving in real work setting	Few, increasing
6	Work-linked group project	1–32	Group working in real work setting	Few, increasing
7	Work-place visit	up to 1	Awareness raising, career taster	Few
8	Simulated case studies	—	Case study experience simulating w-e learning	Few, likely to increase

* not necessarily in a single block (e.g. nursing)

Organised experience relevant to work, external to the programme of study

Organised experience, external to the programme of study involves a small, but growing number of students, who find it a useful experience to include on their *curriculum vitae*. These experiences are of three types (Figure 1.2):

- an organised, planned work setting, usually during the long vacation, designed to provide students with development of employability skills and an introduction to the world of work;

- courses that help develop employability skills;

- work shadowing to provide students with an insight into particular types of jobs.

Figure 1.2 **Organised work experience external to the programme of study (Appendix 1)**

	Type	Typical length	Objectives (for student)	Student participation
9	Structured vacation work (e.g. STEP)	8–12	To get 'relevant' experience and insight	Some (e.g. 1500 on STEP)
10	Work-experience vacation placement	2–10	Taster/potential recruitment vehicle (obtain money)	Some
11	Organised world-wide placements (AIESEC, IAESTE)	—	Widen experience of workplace and other cultures	Rare, limited places
12	Short vacation 'courses', (CRAC, EPSRC)	0.5	Awareness raising, skills training	Quite rare
13	Work shadowing and mentoring	0.5	Awareness raising, career taster	Rare but increasing

Ad hoc work experience external to the programme of study

Ad hoc work experiences are usually those associated with the student undertaking part-time work during term-time or vacation work to earn some money, or voluntary work out of a sense of commitment or interest. They are unrelated, in essence, to programmes of study nor are they linked to any structured programme (Figure 1.3). However, several institutions are beginning to find ways of incorporating these experiences into the programmes of study, not least by crediting voluntary or part-time work as a module of study (Chapter 6).

Figure 1.3 ***Ad hoc* work experience external to the programme of study (Appendix 1)**

	Type	Objectives (for student)	Student participation
14	Traditional vacation work	To earn money	Most
15	Term-time part-time work	To earn money	50%, increasing
16	Working in family business	Obligation /to earn money	Some
17	Voluntary work, term-time	For experience in 'relevant' area or area of interest	Few (decreasing?)
18	Voluntary work, vacations	For experience in 'relevant' area or area of interest	Few (decreasing?)
19	Time off during the programme	Broaden experience/alleviate financial hardship	Rare, increasing
20	Gap year before or after the programme	Broaden experience (obtain money)	Some, increasing

As well as a range of different types of work experience, there is also a range of different perceptions about the usefulness of work experience depending on the ethos and culture of the work-experience provider. This may range from organisations, especially SMEs, who see work experience as an investment for which they require some return, to organisations who consider the provision of work experience opportunities as an altruistic contribution to educational development. Different approaches involve different expectations of work experience and very different experiences for students (Appendix 2).

Summary

- Work experience and related benefits are not a new issue for higher education. Work experience has particular prominence at present because of the rapidly changing nature of organisations and subsequent demands of graduates and because of the profile given to it by Dearing. The research is, thus, examining ways of expanding work experience both in terms of the quantity of opportunities available and the quality of the opportunities.

- A range of stakeholders are involved in work experience and in order to successfully expand there must be a recognition of the parties involved, clear links between the parties and clarification of how each group benefits in the short and long term.

- There is a wide range of work experiences and these are relevant to most types of undergraduates, including:
  - traditional school leavers;
  - full-time, mature students who may have had work experience but not reflected on it;
  - part-time students in work who may need some guidance on reflection and evaluation of work experience in order to add value;
  - part-time unemployed students.

- The range of different forms of work experience can be grouped into three broad categories:
  - organised work experience that is part of a programme of study;
  - organised work experience external to a programme of study;
  - *ad hoc* work experience external to the programme of study;

- The variety of work experience opportunities is paralleled by a range of different perceptions about the efficacy and effectiveness of work experience that relate to the organisational profile of the organisation. An adaptation of the workplace profile (developed in *Graduates' Work*, 1997) provides a framework for exploring the benefits of *work experience* for organisations, students and academic staff in higher education institutions (Appendix 2).

2 Learning and work experience

Experience of work should not be regarded as something that is intrinsically beneficial: something that is somehow 'good for the soul'. On the contrary, it is a means to an end and it is important to keep the end in sight. The end is the learning that comes from the experience.

Work experience offers a significant route to developing a range of graduate attributes and plays an important role in augmenting the higher education learning experience. Work experience is a process that is part of the whole spectrum of learning.

As explored in Chapter 1, work experience can offer the opportunity to develop skills that enable students to be work-ready, that is, be at the adaptive end of the enhancement continuum (Appendix 2, Figure A2.2). However, work experience is not limited to these 'fitting-in', 'adaptive' skills, there is considerable evidence of students developing further along the continuum, developing such skills and abilities as negotiation, persuasion, leadership, and also, importantly, developing as independent learners.

So, as well as seeing work experience within the spectrum of learning, it is also important to recognise that there is a spectrum of learning associated with work experience.

Thus one should avoid the temptation to think that there is only one ideal form of work experience, as different forms may offer different benefits and students may participate in a range of work experiences. This fits in with viewing learning as a transformative process that is not restricted to particular institutions of learning.

The potential learning that comes from work is not limited to the student, there are opportunities for learning by staff involved, both in higher education institutions and employers. For employers, learning associated with developing work experience includes staff developing as mentors and enablers as well as building up links with higher education institutions.

Experience of work, then, is not enough in itself. It is the *learning that comes from it* that is important. This leads to seven interrelated areas that are crucial to work experience:

- 'meaningful' experience;
- intention;
- reflection and articulation;
- assessment;
- accreditation;
- quality monitoring;
- work-experience portfolio.

Meaningful experience

There is an issue about whether any period of working in any setting constitutes *meaningful* work experience. This is an extremely tricky issue. Different stakeholders have different views about what constitutes a meaningful experience.

Academic staff tend to want the work experience to link to the subject specialism or discipline, even if only tenuously. Thus, for example, a sociology student who works in a small enterprise as a clerk is not seen to have a meaningful experience, but if the student initiates an equal opportunity policy, then the experience becomes meaningful. There is a small groundswell from within some higher education institutions that takes the view that work experience is about personal development as much as, or instead of, subject development, but this is still rare.

Employers tend to see meaningful work experience in organisational terms, that is, it is meaningful if the experience is sufficiently structured and of sufficient time for the student to gain an appreciation of the organisation and its culture and to make a positive contribution to the organisation. Some employers expect work experience to relate to the development of job-relevant attributes:

> When I say relevant work experience I don't just mean photocopying, I mean proper concrete stuff. I know that is difficult when you are doing a degree because, from an employer's point of view they are not really going to want to give someone a lot of responsibility who is only going to be there and then go back to their course. So that is easier said than done.
>
> (Office Manager, small private specialist employment agency)

> Well if I can just give you the view of somebody who is not from this country, I am actually amazed by the lack of work experience of the British student. British students are younger than the average – they finish earlier. Therefore, they sometimes don't have the maturity. They have had to take jobs to earn money to support themselves, which didn't bring anything to the equation. They are in direct competition with these people who are 25 and who have gone through meaningful work experience because it is part of their curriculum in the business school or the university. I look at work experience of British students but I very rarely find meaningful work experience.
>
> (Line Manager, large financial institution)

Students tend to have varied views about what is meaningful. Some expect work experience to allow them to put elements of their course into practice. Others expect it to help develop work-related skills. Others look for work experience to help them develop or 'mature' in a broader sense. For some, the financial necessity may be what gives their work experience its meaning. It seems that students who have undertaken work experience, as part of post-school education, tend to value the opportunity as the respondents to the Rover Group (1998) *Young People Development Survey* illustrates (Figure 2.1)

Brokers – those who arrange or mediate work-experience opportunities – often have a funding or initiative agenda, for example developing the local economy. Thus a 'meaningful experience' is often linked to solving a business problem, enhancing SME's productivity or building up beneficial links between higher education and employers.

Figure 2.1   Usefulness of different forms of work experience as perceived by respondents to Rover Group Young People Development Survey, 1997

	Valid resp.	Very useful		Fairly useful		Not very useful		Not useful at all	
	N	n	%	n	%	n	%	n	%
Work experience in year 10 or 11 at school	423	174	41	178	42	52	12	19	4
Work experience at 6th Form college	82	31	38	32	39	14	17	5	6
During vocational course at FE college	31	17	55	8	26	3	10	3	10
During a sandwich course at university	29	25	86	2	7	2	7	0	0
Through Rover's Student Placement Scheme	44	37	84	6	14	1	25	0	0
With another employer while at university	36	26	72	7	19	3	8	0	0
Of part-time, term-time paid work	289	112	38	127	44	43	15	7	2
Of vacation paid employment	119	37	31	61	51	16	13	5	4
Of working in a family business	56	27	48	19	34	9	16	1	2
Of voluntary work in a not-for-profit organisation	39	13	33	18	46	6	15	2	5
Of a structured national/regional scheme (e.g. STEP)	6	3	50	2	33	0	0	1	17
Of taking a year out after school or university	25	17	68	6	24	2	8	0	0

In some forms of work experience professional bodies are also an interested party. Harvey and Mason (1995) suggest that, generally, they have three foci of interest and they can be related to their involvement in work experience:

- the public interest – in which case they act as a watchdog (in a similar way to regulatory bodies but from within the profession);
- the interest of the professional practitioners – where they act as a professional association or trade union (including legitimating restrictive practices), or as a learned society contributing to continuous professional development;
- self interest – where they act to maintain their own privileged position as a controlling body.

There are differences between types of work experience that are related directly to the programme of study and those that are unrelated to the programme of study. Work experience, related to the course, may focus on seeing subject-related theoretical knowledge in practice, alongside the development of other skills, reflecting that course-specific work experience was developed in response to the need for students to apply their learning.

Non-subject related work experience may be more about thinking and doing in terms of generic skills. However, *ad hoc* work experience is very varied and employers often find it difficult to evaluate:

> It depends what they do. If they just go abroad and visit relations they haven't learned anything about life, they have just taken 'plane trips. If they go down into Kurdistan and work for villagers and they really show self-reliance, stand on their own two feet, that's OK. Voluntary Service Overseas, that sort of thing, where they have really done a job of work and they can show what they've learned – because that is really work experience – that's OK.
>
> (Strategic Manager, automobile supply company)

If 'non-traditional' forms of work experience are to be maximised for their learning opportunities, then students need some kind of structure within which to develop as learners. As with all forms of work experience there is a need for students to be supported in their learning so they can recognise and articulate it.

At root, though, for an experience to be meaningful, the student needs to reflect on it and identify what has been learned, which is made easier if the learning is planned and intentional.

Intention

For work experience to become a valuable learning process it needs to be intentional, planned and recognised (Duckenfield and Stirner, 1992). Indeed, the working definition of work experience suggested that it is defined as a period of work that is *designed* to encourage reflection on the experience and to identify the learning that comes from working. It is possible to retrospectively reflect, but as Knapper and Cropley (1985) suggest, lifelong learning is not just about the spontaneous day-to-day learning of everyone's life, rather it is what Tough (1971) terms 'deliberate' learning, key characteristics of which include that it is intentional and has specific goals rather than vague generalisations. Obviously, this principle can be applied to any form of work experience. This transforms work experience into work-based learning.

Viewing work experience as experiential learning identifies the need for ongoing reflection which can be built upon whilst still in the workplace:

> Experiential learning is an integration and an alternation of thinking and doing. It is the method by which effective, progressive and eventually self-directed learning can occur, with all that this means for individual and collective confidence, ability and progress. When the doing and the thinking have been sufficiently iterated, a reliable conclusion is reached and knowledge progresses to understanding... there must be time for learners to selectively critically reflect on their experience, to reach reasoned conclusions or to modify their experience so that further opportunity for learning is given. (Davies, 1990)

Reflection and articulation

Graduates who are able to identify work experience on their *curriculum vitae* are at an advantage, when applying for jobs, over students without some form of work experience. However, although having work experience may once have been a significant factor, it is now the ability to identify what has been learned from the experience that counts. The *articulation* of what has been *learned* is therefore a key issue, and it is imperative that students are supported to enable them to articulate their experiences. Articulation of learning and development is essential for students to be able to communicate their work experience to potential employers.

> I know at interview I was questioned about the work experience I had done and some of it was quite menial but what I had learned was quite significant. So, it is not necessarily how wonderful the job sounds but what you, as an individual, got out of it and put in to it: how it shapes you into something.　　(Marketing Officer, multi-national food manufacturer)

Furthermore, work experience as part of the undergraduate experience is not just about learning for a job, or even a career, or even for employment. What is significant about work experience is development as an independent learner and development of key skills. It is a means towards self-development and interaction in general, not just in a narrow work-place setting. So reflection needs to be seen in a wider sense than reflecting on the development of narrowly-defined, job-relevant skills.

Reflection needs some kind of structure within which the learning can take place and by which students can articulate this to potential employers. A generic model of encouraging reflection on the learning process involves encouraging students to focus on the objectives of their work experience and critically review their own progress at regular intervals throughout. This could take a variety of forms: a handbook with prompts on various key-skill issues, or students could be required to write a reflective essay, or provide a section in their report on the work experience, or use an interactive learning tool such as a CD-ROM.

Students should be prompted to reflect on their experiences and how they feel they have changed as a result of those experiences, rather than simply write down what happened. Ideally, these reflective practices should take place at regular intervals throughout the work experience, so that students can look back and see how their day-to-day experiences gradually shaped their learning and confidence. Through encouraging students to reflect on their learning, students are empowered as lifelong learners. First, they are able to recognise what they have learned. Second, they gain an understanding of how they learn, which they can use to improve their learning effectiveness in the future. Third, they develop the language to describe their achievements to others.

L'Association Internationale des Étudiants en Sciences et Commerciales (AIESEC), Diagio and Marks and Spencer are developing a tool to enable students to record their learning and take a more proactive role in their own development. The 'AIESEC Tracker' encompasses the whole learning experience, including academic experiences, work experience and the range of extra-curricular activities. It aims to provide a 'means of capturing those experiences and learning from them' (AIESEC, 1998). The Tracker encourages students to reflect on current strengths, identify areas for potential learning and development, record and reflect on the learning from events and situations and attend feedback sessions with an advisor to help examine their learning and set future targets.

A wide variety of work experience can, therefore, be made into a 'meaningful' experience through a process of careful reflection. However, as suggested above, the learning is likely to be greater and the quality of the experience higher if the experience is 'intentional and recognised'.

In short, retrospective reflection on an experience can be meaningful in terms of learning and development. However, a well-planned experience, with ongoing and built-in, 'real-time', reflection, linked to identifiable outcomes, is likely to optimise the learning potential. This stresses the need for organisation and preparation of any form of work experience to enable students to maximise the learning opportunities.

Assessment

Focusing on different types of work experience leads on to the issue of assessment. If work experience is to be part of an undergraduate programme, then there is pressure to formally assess it and accredit it towards the degree or a separate internal or external award. If one is to capture learning from work experience that is not part of the programme then there needs to be a structure within which this can take place. Assessment may provide this structure as it is a way of making the learning from work experience intentional and a means by which to encourage on-going reflection. Assessment also provides evidence of learning (Duckenfield and Stirner, 1992), which may be demanded by higher education institutions and employers. Assessment can take a vast range of forms – essential elements are that it involves reflection and that it is not isolated from the rest of the learning process.

A widening of work experience raises four kinds of issues around assessment:

- assessment to make work experience 'valuable' to students (instrumentalism);

- making work experience equivalent to non-work experience (equal amounts of assessed work);

- assessing the development of a range of attributes not just written output (assessing the *experience*);

- shifting the emphasis to give the student more opportunity and responsibility to develop as an independent learner.

Different stakeholders have different objectives in linking assessment to work experience. Students expect to have their development assessed, it can keep up the learning momentum, can provide formative feedback, can act as a motivator for students and can help to diagnose and remedy mistakes (Brown and Knight, 1994, pp. 33–37).

The assessment of work experience offers different challenges to the assessment of some other forms of undergraduate learning as there are more partners involved, and there is the issue of each of the parties' roles in assessment. These are not easy issues to resolve and it is important not to 'bog down' work experience with a heavy burden of conventionally assessed written work. There are, thus, staff-development implications of a widening of assessment.

Employer commitment is key – they must, in some way, be involved in the assessment: the course team need their views on the student. It also means that employers are, and feel, involved in the whole of the work experience.

> *If you took someone to do a project over the Christmas holidays would you then get feedback or provide feedback for that person to the institution?*

> Yes, we give feedback to the University and it is assessed feedback. It's quite terrifying really. It's a fifth of their final year mark so you can't give them the wrong mark. What is horrendous about that is that no-one has ever really given us guidance on how to evaluate someone's performance. I would like to think we are sensible enough to take it seriously but certainly in the early days it would have been less painful if we knew what a 2.1 looked like. (Business Manager, small design and communications company)

There is no requirement that employers be asked to 'grade' work-experience students, even if they are given some insights into the academic grading process. However, employers should normally be asked to provide qualitative evaluation of student development, which may or may not be translated into a summative grade.

Developing forms of supported self-assessment of work experience may be key to developing reflective, critical assessment methods that enhance deep learning and facilitate ongoing reflection and fit into a pattern of lifelong learning. Assessment shapes both the way in which students learn and their experience of learning.

> Assessment is at the heart of the undergraduate experience. Assessment defines what students regard as important, how they spend their time, and how they come to see themselves as students and then as graduates.
>
> (Brown and Knight, 1994, p. 12)

A generic model of the assessment of the learning could centre on the use of self-assessment through reflection in an ongoing way. This would be supported by employers and academics and then perhaps used by the higher education institution to give academic credit (Figure 2.1).

There is a growing pressure for a profile[1] that goes beyond a formal academic learning profile (let alone single summative degree classification) and the impact that will have on the students' motivation to take extra-curricular activities of all kinds more seriously, including work experience, irrespective of formal assessment towards the degree.

Figure 2.1   Model of assessment

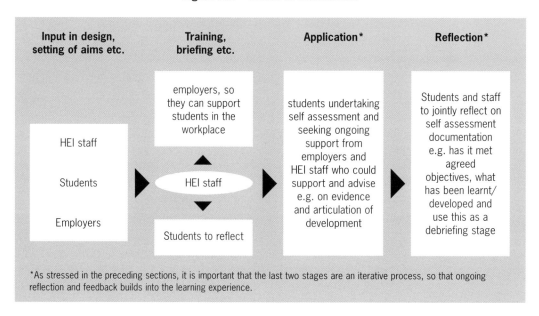

Input in design, setting of aims etc.

HEI staff

Students

Employers

Training, briefing etc.

employers, so they can support students in the workplace

HEI staff

Students to reflect

Application*

students undertaking self assessment and seeking ongoing support from employers and HEI staff who could support and advise e.g. on evidence and articulation of development

Reflection*

Students and staff to jointly reflect on self assessment documentation e.g. has it met agreed objectives, what has been learnt/ developed and use this as a debriefing stage

*As stressed in the preceding sections, it is important that the last two stages are an iterative process, so that ongoing reflection and feedback builds into the learning experience.

Accreditation

Issues of assessment of work experience are clearly linked to the accreditation of the experience. It can be argued that if it is to be taken seriously, work experience needs to be accredited, either towards the programme award or as a separate award of the institution or of an external body.

Little (1997) provides a useful schema of the accreditation of mainly organised work experience:

- *satisfactory completion*, for example, traditional sandwich placement;

- *specific academic credit*, for example, the module that accredits term-time voluntary work at Napier University or the structured work experience at Oxford Brookes University;

- *separate award from the university*, for example certification provided by Loughborough, Ulster, Brunel;

- *separate award of the university and an external qualification*, such as a exemptions from professional body requirements, for example, at the University of Surrey;

- *separate award from an independent body*, for example, City and Guilds licentiateship, NVQ, University of Cambridge Local Examinations Syndicate (for post-16 work experience).

---

1   There is considerable work in progress on this issue of recording student achievement and detailed analysis of it is beyond the scope of this report.

To this we could add accreditation that is given by student unions or by employers such as ASDA 'Flying Start'. The latter involves employers awarding points that can be traded in for training courses. Students have a record of training in the form of a passport which they can take with them or use if they are subsequently employed by ASDA.

Traditionally, the one-year sandwich course tended not to be accredited towards the final qualification *per se*. Students normally had to satisfactorily complete the placement in order to progress or to obtain a sandwich qualification. In most sandwich courses, students are expected to undertake small amounts of coursework during the placement year, which may contribute towards a final classification and students usually produce an undergraduate project, in their final year, linked to the placement year. However, skills and abilities developed on the placement tend not to be assessed, only written products based, in part, on the placement as a case study. This situation is changing and some universities are assessing skills developed during placement.

There are a number of issues that relate to the importance of accreditation to the different parties involved including the following:

- Do students only take work experience seriously if it is accredited?
- Is it the qualifications *per se* that employers favour or the fact that students have undertaken work experience and reflected and learned from it?
- Do employers favour particular forms of accreditation?

There is the argument that students start out by being motivated by external accreditation of work experience, for example, by City and Guilds, but end up more motivated by the process of reflection than by the ultimate gain of an externally accredited certificate.

There seems to be little hard evidence that employers are concerned that work experience is accredited – it is, as suggested above, that students have *reflected* on it and can *articulate* their learning that is important. Where accreditation has occurred, there is some anecdotal evidence that employers give more credence to nationally recognised accreditation rather than institutional certificates.

Quality monitoring

Ultimately, work experience must be a 'quality' process. The quality of the work experience is thus intrinsically tied to its relevance, structure, organisation and intentionality.

> I would like to do more regular summer vacation or summer placements or industrial placements with one of the design colleges. We haven't done anything more formal because I feel that it needs investment from us as much as the person who is coming here and we have been so busy that I wouldn't have felt happy doing it because I just don't think we are actually giving them anything. It's all very well saying, yes, come along for a placement and then sit in the corner for three weeks because I actually can't give you any input. I think it is very important that places are organised, that they are properly organised. And that there is a structure to it and there is a 'what do you want to learn, what can I give you?'.
>
> (Design Manager, small design and communications)

If work experience is to be a quality experience then employers must be committed to it and be fully aware of the implications. They need to be involved in the planning and share the responsibility for success, which means ensuring the work experience student is provided with adequate, trained and supportive supervision.

> I think one of the main problems that I had with the whole placement was that the guy who was actually in charge of me didn't have a great deal of experience of working with graduates and couldn't really give me a great deal of guidance or consistency of work.
>
> (Performance Analyst, large freight company)

Similarly, academic staff must have an ongoing responsibility to monitor and support the work-experience students. It is not just a matter of 'placing' students but ensuring that students recognise their learning experience. Thus, students also have an active role which entails both responsibility for their own development and also the power to be able to shape this development.

> I did work experience on my degree and I spent a year making cups of tea and photocopying. So that experience is neither here nor there. In theory, if it was good experience it would count in recruitment. But the experience you get on a lot of sandwich courses isn't very good.
>
> (Office Manager, small private specialist employment agency)

It is important to reiterate, what many experienced practitioners know, that the quality of work experience is greatly enhanced by the following:

- prior induction and briefing of all concerned;
- facilitation of ongoing reflection;
- debriefing and identification of outcomes.

Familiarisation and briefing

A prior briefing or period of familiarisation is essential to ensure that all parties are clear what is expected of them, what are the objectives of the work experience, so that students are not just 'thrown in at the deep end'.

A prior briefing also establishes an ongoing dialogue between the different parties, which can be utilised and developed throughout the relationship.

> If I look at the placement, that works nicely because we actually got together, we sat down with some representatives from the [University], and together we designed a training plan for the placement scheme. I felt that was excellent because we got to know about them, they got to know about us, and we worked together so the student was getting the most out of their year. Perhaps if we could think of ways of transferring some of that into other graduate recruitment that would be a start.
>
> (Line Manager, medium-sized insurance company)

Learners need to consider what they already know, what they intend to learn, how they will achieve this and how they will demonstrate or prove this. In essence, this is best achieved through using learning contracts. Essentially a learning contract involves a three-way agreement between the student, the employer and the academic, on the objectives, practices and outcomes of the work experience. A formal arrangement may be less achievable for students undertaking *ad hoc* work experience, and in such cases a pseudo learning contract could be used through negotiation between the student and for example, an academic. If, for example, students are utilising the learning from term-time, part-time work this kind of objective setting may be after the work has commenced.

It is important to ensure that the familiarisation and briefing takes place in an overt and positive manner.

> There should be greater support from the university and training officers at the beginning of the placement to ensure that everything is settled and the placement objectives are clear and achievable.
>
> (CRQ, 1997, respondent no.49)

In Computing Science at the University of Glasgow students undertake a placement for 10 weeks in the summer vacation between their third and fourth year. Each project has a clearly defined set of goals against which progress can be measured by the student, the employer and the supervisor.

Volunteers undertaking international projects through GAP have to go through an induction programme that includes a pre-placement presentation at GAP House based on the country in which the volunteers are undertaking the projects. The presentation is run by a project manger and also involves discussion with returning volunteers. Volunteers are also given a very detailed briefing.

However, there are some situations, such as emotional trauma in medicine and other health-related disciplines, for which it is particularly difficult to prepare and only through having the experience can students learn to deal with these situations.

Ongoing monitoring and supporting ongoing reflection

There needs to be ongoing reflection by the learner, and ongoing support and reflection from employers and academics in higher education institutions, as well as from any fourth party. This is a key part of experiential learning as an iterative process.

On-going reflection is essential at all stages: at the beginning (as outlined above), whilst undertaking work experience so students can alternate reflection and experience, and at the end so that students may subsequently build on the learning, take it forward and integrate it into the rest of their learning.

Ongoing reflection can be facilitated by ongoing supervision, which in course-related work experience may involve continual three-way dialogue and feedback.

> The only feedback was the supervisors who visited here periodically. It tends to be that the supervisor used to arrive once a term and that was it – the student was placed and then went away again. If I was looking to taking on placements then I would want more contact, liaison, discussion with the institution than I saw previously. I don't know if I'd take placements on unless I thought that they and ourselves had got better dialogue.
>
> (Research Manager, small private research organisation)

On the supervised work experience, which is part of the Hotel and Restaurant Management Degree at Oxford Brookes University, a self-development document is used. This provides specific information for the student to help them to conceptualise the role the placement will have in their learning and in their degree course, and to help them to prepare for the pro-active, reflective learning process. The aim of the self-development programme is to: 'facilitate student learning by encouraging you to take advantage of challenging opportunities in both professional and personal life' (OBUSHRM, 1997, p. 6). The student is expected to direct their own learning throughout the placement by making a series of learning agreements, which are later included in the portfolio along with their outcomes. Students also prepare a reflective journal, to help them consolidate their learning and track their progress. The ongoing reflection throughout the process also provides the opportunity for identifying and rectifying any potential problems any party is having with the work experience and, in the worst case scenario, the opportunity to terminate the work experience.

Debriefing

Debriefing continues the process of dialogue. For many students, work experience is not followed up by timely or adequate debriefing. They are often not asked for feedback, let alone exposed to a structured debriefing of their experiences.

Debriefing needs to be for all parties, students, higher education institutions and also employers who often feel they are not asked for feedback or that they do not receive feedback.

> I don't hear from them much. I may be the wrong person here and it may well be that my boss, for example, would get regular questionnaires but nobody then asks me what I think about them. When we have taken people on placements and I have been the manager of those people, I have had to fill in forms. We had somebody recently who was very bright and I think she will go a long way. She came back to see us afterwards and asked if anyone had 'phoned us to check if she had been here and they hadn't. If I hadn't filled in the form there would be no record at all. She need not have turned up, she could have been swanning round Europe for all they knew.
>
> (Specialist Journalist Manager, large public broadcasting organisation)

Feedback is sometimes formalised, such as the exit questionnaires of employers and students used in the STEP programme. At Oxford Brookes the course team send forms to the employers, with the students' comments, and employers are invited to feed back, completing the full circle of monitoring

Work-experience portfolio

It is important to recognise that there are a range of potential work experience opportunities. So, it is important that staff, students and employers should not think solely in terms of any one particular type of work experience and disregard other possibilities. Similarly, stakeholders should not consider 'work experience' as a homogeneous, undifferentiated whole. Instead, staff should encourage, employers should look for, and students develop a *work-experience portfolio*.

> I had some work experience at the refinery previously as a summer student. Before that I had worked at ICI and Procter and Gamble as an undergraduate. I did a pre-university year at ICI and then did a summer course there and, also, in my final summer I did a ten-week placement with Procter and Gamble.
>
> (Recent graduate, multi-national petro-chemical company)

The notion of a work-experience portfolio, simple as it is in essence, is a significant step from the initial recommendation in *Graduates' Work*, which emphasised the year-long placement. While the year placement is a model with enormous benefits, it is not the only model, nor is it feasible, in the short run, to expect there to be enough year-long placements to meet demand.

The important thing is to have a variety of experiences and to be able to reflect on the learning that comes from them:

> Well the sort of people who apply to us, you would be amazed what they have packed in. They may have been on a CRAC course or they may have made Industrial Society presentations or they may have been on a Christmas course with a company or they have done a summer vacation placement, or they have had a gap year where they have done something. One of the benefits of kids having to work their way through, is that whilst they may have been at Tesco, Tesco would quickly realise that they had a bit of a gem here and so they become team leader on the shelf stacking on the nightshift or something, and so the kids can draw from that and draw attention to it as part of their leadership experience.
>
> (Vice-President, multi-national food manufacturers)

It is important that students are encouraged to build up links between the different forms of work experience they undertake, so they are not seen as isolated pockets of learning. Rather the learning from one experience may input into the next experience.

Mature students may have different requirements of work experience whilst they are undergraduates. This may include issues such as reflection on work undertaken before they became a student in order to be able to recognise the learning and articulate it. This does not mean that they should not also undertake work experience whilst being a student but it would help to identify their particular needs from the potential experiences and to complement the range of experiences they have already. Careers-service staff have a key role to play here.

Work experience and lifelong learning

In the same way as recognising that there is a range of learning associated with a range of work experiences, we must also recognise that this learning forms part of the spectrum of experiences in lifelong learning.

Learning is the key focus of work experience and the learning of all parties involved should be maximised. Organisations that recognise and develop as learning organisations through realising the potential of work experience can be seen as taking a transformative, stakeholder-flexible approach to the workplace. This involves a recognition that learning is an ongoing experience, which is not restricted to educational institutions nor is it restricted to work experience.

The key, and simple, idea of the learning society is that a person's initial education and training will be insufficient to meet the needs of working life. Most people will have several rather than single careers. The nature of jobs will change dramatically. Only by continuous learning throughout their working life will individuals remain employable and societies competitive. And continuous learning requires two things: 1) capacity and motivation; 2) the provision of accessible learning opportunities within society.   (Brennan and Little, 1996)

Learning organisations are those that encourage workers to continue learning throughout their working lives. Adapting to changes is crucial for success in the changing world. A commitment to learning is evident, in many organisations, by their approach to higher education: getting involved; sustaining links with higher education institutions and providing placement opportunities for students.

Work experience in a learning organisation is not just about the provision of opportunities. It involves ensuring that the student is given support (in various ways) while they are in the workplace so that students can have a meaningful learning experience, while doing a real job, and develop as independent learners. It is about seeing this learning as a continuous process.

We try and set out very clearly to people, through all manner of means, conventional means like brochures, university visits, through visits to individual departments, and through summer work experience what the form of development will be for the young people joining the company within the first three years. We have a development process because that's the way people need to develop to remain employable by us and by others. What we try and learn together is what we need to know to remain distinctive as a company. We have these programmes of early development that give young people coming in the opportunity to continue to develop their specialist skills. These programmes will seek to provide the buttressing skills, the allied skills that they won't have had necessarily in a university course, but are essential for them to communicate with their fellow men and women in the company, and to understand what's going on around them. There will be training and development and experience in this broad field of business awareness and in specific areas, like finance, where appropriate, and there will be all sorts of encouragement and opportunity for them to learn to work together.

(Strategic Manager, multi-national petro-chemical company)

Learning in the higher education setting is one part of a lifelong process of learning. Knapper and Cropley's (1985) definition of life-long learning stresses the importance of the learning potential of the workplace.

Summary

- Experience of work should not be regarded as something that is intrinsically beneficial, it is a means to an end and it is the learning that comes from the work experience that is important. Work experience is a process that is part of the whole spectrum of learning. However, there is also a spectrum of learning associated with work experience.

- There is no agreement on what constitutes a *meaningful* work experience. Academic staff tend to want the work experience to link to the subject specialism. Employers tend to see it as meaningful if it allows students to gain an appreciation of the organisation and to make a positive contribution. Students expect work experience to provide a practical context for their study, to develop skills, or provide a setting in which they 'mature'.

- For an experience to be meaningful, the student needs to *reflect* on it and identify what has been learned. It is imperative that students are supported to enable them to articulate their experiences and critically review their own progress at regular intervals. Through encouraging students to reflect on their learning, students are empowered as lifelong learners.

- The learning is likely to be greater and the quality of the experience higher if the experience is *intentional* and recognised. Retrospective reflection on an experience can be meaningful but a well-planned experience, with ongoing and built-in reflection, linked to identifiable outcomes, is likely to optimise the learning potential. This stresses the need for organisation and preparation of any form of work experience to enable students to maximise the learning opportunities.

- If work experience is to be part of an undergraduate programme, then there is pressure to formally *assess* it. Assessment shapes the way in which students learn and their experience of learning. However, assessment for such purposes tends to be commentary upon the work experience rather than direct assessment of attributes or task effectiveness.

- Issues of assessment of work experience are clearly linked to the *accreditation* of the experience: either towards the programme award or as a separate award of the institution or of an external body. However, it is not clear that students only take work experience seriously if it is accredited, nor is it clear whether employers value such accreditation.

- Ultimately work experience must be a *quality* process and a structure that encourages briefing of students, ongoing reflection by students and debriefing has been widely used in developing quality work-experience opportunities. The quality of the work experience is thus intrinsically tied to its relevance, structure, organisation and intentionality.

- Students should be encouraged to develop a *work-experience portfolio*, taking in a range of different types of work experience.

There appear to be three key areas for the potential expansion of work experience opportunities, which are explored in detail in the following chapters:

- embedded work experience, particularly encouraging the involvement of SMEs (Chapter 3);

- project-linked experience as either a part of a programme of study or as a vacation activity brokered by external bodies (Chapter 4);

- recognition of term-time, part-time and traditional vacation work (Chapter 5).

3 Embedded work-experience

This chapter will explore the potential for expanding work experience embedded in the programme of study. The chapter will, first, examine the benefits for employers, students and staff in higher education institutions of traditional sandwich placements and short course-embedded work experience opportunities (Appendix 1). It will then explore barriers to expanding provision and suggest some ways of overcoming these barriers.

What is embedded work experience

Embedded work experience includes traditional sandwich placements and short periods of work experience as part of the programme of study.

The traditional year-long sandwich placement, either for an academic or calendar year, is often viewed as the exemplary form of work placement, combining a long period of immersion in the work-place setting with course relevance and well-developed structures of support and monitoring of the experience.

Shorter periods of work experience as part of the programme of study take two forms. First, the well-established 'thin' sandwich approach used in professional education and training, which consists of periods of work in different professional settings as part of the undergraduate experience, such as in medical, nursing, social work and other similar degree courses. This is essentially linked to the development of competence to practice. It is not a major focus of this chapter, as expansion of such opportunities is tied to expansion of professional education places.

The second type of short-term, course-embedded work experience includes:

- semester or term-length placements, on a full-time or part-time basis that stand in lieu of modules of study and are assessed towards the final degree award;

- very short, taster placements, usually less than a month, designed to introduce students to a relevant, potential world of work, such as a two-week placement with a radio station for students on a media studies degree programme.

The benefits of course embedded work experience

Benefits to employers

Sandwich placements have become a significant part of the higher education experience, so much so that the term 'placement' tends to be used synonymously with other work-experience opportunities. The well-established traditional year-long, single-block, sandwich placements are particularly valued by employers. For example, in *Graduates' Work* many employers identified the one-year structured placement as the best opportunity to benefit from work experience (Harvey, Moon and Geall, 1997).

> What we were looking for is analytical skills, and are looking for the courses to provide us with those skills. We look favourably on sandwich students because, obviously, they have got work experience. (Research and Information Manager, medium-sized community health authority)

Some employers discover that there are benefits in taking on placement students and that students who have done a period of work placement have an edge when applying for posts:

We have recently taken on some placement people who are doing these new degrees where they have to do the third year with the company, as part of their degree, and it is very recent for [our firm] to do this. I think that they have got an excellent opportunity in their degree to actually spend a year out in industry, because those people, when they apply back, show that little bit more understanding of work, what it is all about, a little bit more appreciation of people and how to work with all sorts of ages, all kinds of things like that. Those that come straight from university, without any experience of work, are at a slight disadvantage and I think it comes across at interview.

(Line Manager, medium-sized insurance company)

As well as the direct benefit of the work undertaken by a sandwich or short-term placement student, employers also benefit in a variety of other ways. Embedded work experience, for example, can be a useful recruitment tool.

I am trying to increase the amount of placements that we offer so that we can recruit a cadre of graduates that we have already had, who have already gone through that pain. Also because we feel it checks out in terms of 'Do we like you?'. We have already seen you for 12 weeks, and, more importantly, 'do you like us from what you have seen on a placement, is this the sort of organisation that you think you want to belong to?'. We have a view that ultimately 50% of our graduate recruits would have come in via the placement route. Certainly, in some of the very technical jobs in the labs they would actively look to recruit people who had been there in the summer or maybe on an industrial placement.

(Recruitment and Development Manager, large telecommunications company)

The longer the placement the more that the employer and the student can learn about each other and the more they are able to gauge suitability for future employment. As a recruitment tool, the traditional one-year placement can be seen as less risky than other methods. First, employers have the opportunity to judge the performance of undergraduates over a long period of time. In addition, the placement route aids the retention of new recruits because students know by the end of a year whether they really want to work for their host organisation.

The objective is to have them for placement with a view to recruiting them. It is done for two reasons. One, because they can be contributing something that otherwise we would have to get subcontractors in to do. Two, because the best assessment process is a one-year long experience with the individual and it works in both directions, we can assess them and they can assess us.

(Personnel Director, multi-national engineering company)

Guinness, for example, have recognised the potential for sandwich placements and other work experience schemes that form a part of their human resources strategy. Their strategy to recruit through placements rather than through a traditional graduate recruitment scheme has enabled them to cut their costs substantially (Cook, 1997).

Marks and Spencer have substantial experience of providing six- and twelve-month placements for students. They report that 40% of students on their scheme are subsequently offered employment with the firm. There are many other large employers of graduates investing and benefiting from such schemes. For some organisations, recruitment is built into the placement opportunity:

What happens is, they join us for a year, we place them in the businesses in roles of a grade directly below assistant manager. That is for a year and it could be anywhere from a branch to a mortgaging department. They are recruited on a similar process to the [fast-track graduate trainees]. Throughout that year they go into the same appraisal processes as any member of the organisation. At the end of that year, if the line manager feels that their performance has been of a high enough level of quality, and we give them guidelines there, the person can be recommended for a place on the fast-track graduate selection centre the following year, which means that they miss out all the previous stages of the process and come straight in at selection-centre stage. Their experience in the year, and the fact that they have achieved that recommendation, should mean that they have a very good chance of being successful on the selection centre.   (Graduate Recruitment Manager, large financial institution)

In other circumstances, often in smaller organisations, placements lead to serendipitous recruitment:

One of our existing management accountants did come to us as a sandwich placement a few years ago, and went back to finish her degree and then came back to work for us after that. It is not something that is built into our structure, albeit I could see a role for that if the funds were there to support it.   (Director of Financial Services, small housing association)

However, it is not surprising that there are fewer smaller employers to have gained from the experience of providing placements. A recent survey of SMEs found that although only 15% of their sample had experience of recruiting ex-placement or vacation students to their full-time workforce, they believed that this method of recruitment was 'an effective and economic way of recruiting future employees' (Williams and Owen, 1997).

The general experience has been that people coming here are going on their degrees because its the first step of their career path. We do very well out of those I think. They are very positive experiences on both sides. We have benefited in that our last placement student, whom we have recruited, got very specific training relevant to us during that part of his course and has come back now and we have someone who could step in without requiring any additional training.   (Chief Executive, small medical lasers manufacturer)

Course-embedded work experience also offers the opportunity for closer links between employers and higher education, as each get a glimpse of a different context, through the arrangements necessary to set up the work situation for the student. The traditional sandwich placement, for example, provides an ideal opportunity for employers and academics to establish long-term relationships and potential for working together to discuss developments in both spheres.

Links with academic institutions through placements are being used by many employers to help promote and reinforce a learning culture within organisations. Furthermore, employers who invest in a placement culture stand to gain a healthy return in terms of the enthusiasm and new ideas that students bring with them.

Benefits to students

Students can benefit from embedded work experience in a number of ways particularly by developing an appreciation of the work setting, developing 'employability' skills and having the opportunity to put their programme-based knowledge into practice. These learning opportunities are accentuated in the traditional sandwich course because of its extended length and structured academic and practical programme (ASET, 1996).

Although there are many variations in the length, and the ways in which the work-experience element is organised, embedded work experience is recognised as a significant channel for student learning. Indeed, the traditional sandwich placement is more geared than any other form of work experience to drawing out the learning from the workplace setting.

Sandwich education and training, and more generally, work-based learning is a means to an end, not an end in itself. The end, the objective, is to increase the employability of our students, the fact now recognised and accepted as an objective in itself and a cause for celebration.   (Wagner, 1997)

A major benefit of course-embedded work experience is its relevance to the programme of study. Students who have the opportunity to experience a work setting as part of their course potentially benefit in terms of learning to apply their subject knowledge in a general work setting.

The student learning experience is enhanced through the application of theory and the development of practical skills in a work environment. In particular, a sandwich course offers the student the advantage of learning how to reflect on their experience, not just what they have learned, but how they learn. This, in turn, helps students to become more confident and leads to improvements in their academic work. Recent placement students report 'putting theory into practice' as one of the key benefits of their 'sandwich' experience and some felt more motivated for the final year (CRQ, 1997).

The development of a variety of skills in a relevant work context is a key benefit for students who have undertaken a sandwich placement. Students reported that they had developed a number of 'employability' skills while on placement. Of these, the most frequently mentioned were time-management, organisation and self-discipline as well as IT skills and self-confidence (CRQ, 1997). This coincides with perceptions of employers who see periods of embedded work experience as providing an appreciation of the rigours of the working environment:

> The young fellow we have got on placement here talks about working ten hours a week at university. When they come out of university and start working in a company it must be like running into a brick wall for a whole day, because suddenly they are expected to be at work. Suddenly they have to think they have to do this job without a break. The first day must seem like a week. That isn't a bad thing as he has had a marvellous indication of what working for a dynamic and hardworking company is all about.
>
> (Production Director, medium-sized refractory materials manufacturer)

The development of interactive skills, such as communication and team working that are highly valued by employers (Harvey, Moon and Geall, 1997) were also mentioned by sandwich students (CRQ, 1997) as one of the most valuable aspects of their placement experience. In many cases, students on placement will have the opportunity to participate in company appraisals so they will get a sense, from employers, of how they are progressing over a period of time.

Another main benefit that students gained is 'an insight into a career' (CRQ, 1997). A prolonged period of time spent in a workplace setting provides students with a valuable opportunity to 'test the water' (ASET, 1996). Whilst other types of work experience opportunities may also provide this, a longer placement duration enables them to get a real sense of what the organisation and the industry is like, rather than a brief 'snapshot' view.

> I was on a sandwich course and did an industrial placement year. It was a really good year, we were helped to find a job, they didn't necessarily expect very much from you when you got to the placement, but when they did find out what I was like they gave me plenty of work and I learned quite a lot from that. I ended up in a food company for my placement and that was a definite help in interviews, in getting a job in another food company. I had something to draw on, I knew about hygiene and some of the other aspects of food processing.
>
> (Process Engineer, multi-national food manufacturer)

An extended period of work experience is also an invaluable attribute when applying for employment in some areas of work. Students who have undertaken a placement year are well-regarded by graduate recruiters and have an increased likelihood of obtaining employment compared to peers who have no placement experience. Furthermore, one of the advantages of a longer placement is time to build relationships that may turn out to be valuable contacts for the future.

> A placement enables you to get the job when you come out of university, because a lot of places ask what practical experience you have. If you have done a year's sandwich course you have got much better practical skills than somebody having come straight out of university. It's also a fantastic way to get a foot in the door to boost your job prospects when you actually do graduate.
>
> (Trainee Solicitor, large law firm)

There is a good deal of evidence that suggests that students often secure a job offer from the placement (CSU-AGCAS-IER, 1996). The University of Derby estimates that 'around a third of Business Studies students return to the company, in which they did their placement, for their first 'proper' job after university' (University of Derby, 1997). Not only do placement students have a better chance of being employed, they are also more likely to be able to command higher starting salaries (ASET, 1996).

Graduate recruiters also value the placement experience because applicants are better able to articulate and provide evidence of key skills:

> I think both skills and the intangible maturity element are significantly improved by work placements. When we use graduate assessment centres we are looking for evidence of leadership and management skills. Generally, those people who have worked in organisations previously have a host of examples of experiences that they are able to share with us and that makes them stronger candidates in terms of being able to exhibit certain skill bases than those who have just gone to school, higher education and then come straight to us.
>
> (Senior Manager, large financial institution)

Finally, in some circumstances, students benefit financially through paid placements, which, in the past, have often provided students with greater income than a combined grant and earnings from part-time or holiday work. Furthermore, some schemes may lead to sponsorship through the final year. According to the recent CRQ survey, the average gross monthly earnings of students while on a sandwich placement is around £770 and range from £246–£1041. These earnings make a favourable contribution to a student's income and enable many to become financially independent from their parents (CRQ, 1997).

Benefits to staff in higher education institutions

Traditional sandwich placements usually involve a well-established model of quality assurance (see below), albeit marginal to the teaching quality assessment, and, for many academics, such placements provide the optimum learning experience. Indeed, the quality procedures that are supposed to operate for sandwich placement students are often seen as the exemplar against which the quality of other work-experience opportunities should be measured.

> The benefits of ultimate employability derive not only from the sandwich element itself but from the combination of the whole course.
>
> (Brewer, 1997b)

In many cases, academic staff have witnessed increased maturity, motivation and confidence when students return to academic study following a long period of time on placement. Students share their experiences and are more willing to participate in discussions, which enhances the learning environment. Students often get higher marks in their dissertation. In some cases, the impact can be 'dramatic' with students who otherwise would not have been high flyers 'blossoming' as a result of their placement experience (Paddon-Smith, 1997).

> If you were to talk to our current or past students... in excess of 90% will say that the sandwich year was the most important part of the course, they learnt a huge amount on placement, it increased their motivation for the final year, they started to understand what the course was all about, and things like that. You can see, year by year, that the level of academic performance in the final year increases significantly compared to the second year because of the increased motivation and increased contextualisation and general understanding of what the subject area is all about.
>
> (Lee, 1997)

Academic staff at Robert Gordon University were among many who felt that the 'marrying' of theory to practice was the main benefit of embedded work experience. Through the liaison with host organisations, up-to-date practice could be brought into a learning situation and this could be used to inform curriculum development (Jardine and Earl, 1997).

Meaningful and intended experience

It is almost taken as axiomatic that course-embedded work experience, particularly long periods of placement, constitute meaningful work experience. In practice, there are cases where individual placements have been less than satisfactory because they added very little to the particular student's learning. However, staff in higher education institutions involved in sandwich placements usually have little doubt that they constitute a meaningful experience linked to intended learning outcomes. Institutional staff tend to be a little more ambivalent about the value of the learning from shorter periods, with very short placements being seen as nothing much more than awareness-raising events.

The benefits to students that accrue from placements are well documented and the evidence from the *Graduates' Work* (Harvey, Moon and Geall, 1997) research was that, overwhelmingly, students who had experienced placements of any kind considered them to be meaningful experiences. This is a perception echoed in the Rover Group's (1998) *Young People's Development Survey*, which found that 86% of those who had experienced sandwich years found the experience very useful (Figure 2.1). The CRQ (1997) survey of sandwich students further reinforces this endorsement of the process.

Despite the occasional failure, employers on the whole have little doubt that embedded work experience is a meaningful process and one they would like to see extended (Harvey, Moon and Geall, 1997).

> We have had a student from a sandwich course for a year, who took his year out and worked with us. That wasn't too successful, I must admit, but it wouldn't stop us from doing it again.
>
> (General Manager, small medical lasers manufacturer)

Employers tend to consider longer, rather than shorter, periods of work placement as more meaningful. The Executive of the Association of Graduate Recruiters, for example, expressed the view that work experience for a duration of less than six months is too short for both employers and students to gain a meaningful outcome (AGR Executive, 1997). Over a six- or twelve-month period, employers have time to establish relationships, not just with students, but with staff in their academic institutions.

> If companies like ourselves had somebody perhaps for one year then they might be able to do something useful with them, because then you can train them and get something out of them. Any shorter is a waste of time. But then you have to work out who is going to pay for that, does the company pay them, does the university pay them a grant, or whatever?
>
> (Marketing Manager, small journal publishers)

Reflection

Most embedded work experience is clearly linked to a process of reflection as it usually requires students to keep learning diaries or learning logs that are structured in such a way that the students think about how they learn, rather than just what they learn. Students on placements are also often required to undertake coursework that encourages reflection or to use the placement experience as the basis for an undergraduate project.

In addition, many sandwich placements involve 'call-back' days in which students return to the higher education institution for the day to reflect on and discuss their experiences with tutors and peers.

Quality

It is possible that the reputation of the sandwich placement is what makes it such an attractive model for employers. In many instances, course-embedded experiences have well-developed quality mechanisms and forms of assessment, which often involve clear learning objectives, preparation, ongoing support and de-briefing for students and employers (see Chapter 2).

These elements of this model are easily transferable to shorter, less traditional forms of work experience.

Practice in 'managing' the placement process is varied, though there is evidence that many institutions have attempted to co-ordinate institution-wide policies to promote good practice. Other organisations such as the Association of Sandwich Education and Training (ASET) and the British Association of Business Studies Industrial Placements (BABSIP) exist to promote good practice. Models of good practice are also to be found in many discipline areas, notably where courses are validated by, or linked with, professional bodies such as, nursing, radiography and social work.

It is very important, for a quality experience, that placements of any length are adequately supported academically and administratively by appropriately trained staff. In some places, there is institutional pressure to cut back on the tutoring service, which will have adverse effects on the quality of the experience.

The best models to be found are where a significant investment of resources is made, that is, where the resources intended to support placements, actually do just that. There is evidence of good practice in this area. However, adequate support is not cheap:

> If I could just give you an illustration – this is a quick calculation off the top of my head – if we put 150 students out on placement, each one has to be visited three times. In terms of staff time to do the visits, we allow one hour per week as the teaching time equivalent for an academic to visit three students over a year. So for 150 students, you need 50 x 1 hour of an academic's time. If typically H.E. academics do 15 hours of teaching or teaching equivalent time per week, you are talking about 3.3 academics to visit students on placement. The typical cost of employing an academic, with all the overheads, is in the region of £40-60,000 per annum, so the staffing cost of visiting 150 students is somewhere in excess of £150,000, and to that has to be added travel costs, administrative support etc. In addition to that is the cost of placing the students and management of the overall process. So you can see it is not cheap; all told, my best estimate is that it is costing us about £400,000 to run the placement activity for 150 students per year. This is about £2650 per student, of that order, that is about what we receive in income for a sandwich student during the placement year; in fact we receive slightly less than that. (Lee, 1997)

Clearly the cost of the Huddersfield operation is high, but the resources that are invested reflect a commitment to the provision of well-supported placements for students.

On some courses, there is a period of work placement abroad. In the relatively new area of Tourism and Hospitality, international placements are increasingly becoming an integral part of courses. When 'placing' students overseas, it is essential that students are adequately and successfully monitored to ensure that maximum benefit accrues from the placement (Hodgson, 1997).

Familiarisation and briefing

The elements of good 'placement' practice can be seen as the built-in features of course design necessary to optimise the learning opportunities for students. Most sandwich arrangements ensure that students are well prepared for their placement. This often involves a period of pre-placement training[1] followed by meetings between students, employers and higher education staff prior to a period of familiarisation.

All parties need to have clear learning objectives embodied in a contract so that they all know what their responsibilities are, and in particular, the student is encouraged to anticipate their learning. It is essential that the students are involved in any negotiations to get some sense of ownership and take responsibility for their own learning.

---

1   Which, in practice, tends to be of variable length and effectiveness, but further analysis is beyond the scope of this report.

Ongoing monitoring and supporting ongoing reflection

Placement arrangements, in principle, usually involve ongoing support both in the workplace and from the university. Again the quality of this is variable in practice.

> My placement tutor was a complete dickhead. He just didn't listen to you, he talked constantly. He was just more worried about people not being placed, so he would try and fit anyone in anywhere. (Graduate Recruitment Consultant, small private specialist employment agency)

Ideally, there need to be mechanisms built in to the whole process that encourage reflection on the students' learning.

Debriefing

Debriefing students after their placements is an important part of the quality process. As with other forms of work experience this element is often the one that is underdeveloped. Debriefing often 'falls down the cracks' as the timing of placements is such they tend to end as vacations begin. It is often unclear who should be responsible for conducting the debriefing. Even if it is done, the time lag is often too long for effective emotional debriefing. Capturing particular nuances is also difficult after a delay as they become assimilated into taken-for-granteds.

Assessment and accreditation of course-embedded work experience

Reflection and the development of specific learning outcomes is likely to be taken more seriously if the placement is formally recognised and assessed as part of the degree. This takes a variety of forms. The traditional, long, sandwich placement is, as suggested in Chapter 2, often 'assessed' in terms of whether it has been satisfactorily completed, thus enabling the award of a sandwich degree. It is not often assessed towards the degree classification as such. However, there is a growing tendency to include work done during the placement year, or based on the placement year, as part of the assessed array of coursework.

Shorter periods of work placement are also usually assessed, particularly if they are substituting for academic modules. The assessment tends to be based on essays written about the placement experience, evaluations of learning logs or projects undertaken during the placement.

Very short embedded 'taster' experiences tend not to be assessed towards the final award.

There is a growing view that the placement should be based on a clearly defined set of objectives that focus on the learning and development of the student. In addition, it should be an integrated part of the degree linking into the units that are taught both before and after the placement. Furthermore, it should also 'be assessed as part of the degree and influence the final degree classification' (Edmunds, Carter and Lindsay, 1997).

Barriers to expansion of course-embedded work experience

Resources

There are many examples of institutions having increasing difficulties in finding placements, both in the public and private sectors. This is largely the result of economic constraints faced by employers (Jardine and Earl, 1997). The CBI, who were asked by the Dearing Committee to look at ways of increasing the amount of work experience, have stated that:

> There is clearly a problem for the employers who are operating within tight economic constraints. It is recognised that sandwich placements constitute an important form of work experience; however, they are but one manifestation of this and shorter periods of employment such as vacation work can also be useful to employers and students alike.
>
> (Davies, 1997)

There are fears among academics that the scope for substantial expansion of the one-year placement is severely limited as 'there is a limit to the number companies are able to offer' (Milligan, 1997).

Employers have faced unprecedented changes in recent years. Large manufacturers, for example, have less capability than they used to have. There are few large employers who have not undergone significant 'restructuring' in one form or another in recent years. However, in this rapidly changing world, employers have to be pragmatic and many employers have shown renewed commitment to providing work-experience opportunities for students.

However, there may be room for expansion of year placements, particularly in SMEs who do not have placement students at all. Some form of incentive may be needed to initiate the process.

> Government may have to consider tax incentives or new legislation on accounting practices, which will encourage more employers and particularly small and medium employers to become more actively involved in the provision of work experience.   (Brewer, 1997a)

While there may be up-front costs, as many employers have recognised, once the initial costs are invested, repeat years cost less time and effort. Once a placement culture is established, there are substantial benefits to be gained. Marks and Spencer are actively encouraging their supply chain to adopt a placement policy (DfEE, 1997). This may be a significant way forward. There are many large employers with years of experience that could be shared with smaller employers with little or no experience. Williams and Owen (1997) suggest that 'there may be scope for raising awareness amongst employers of the benefits graduates could bring to their businesses'.

The resource issue, it seems, is widespread among all stakeholders. However, research carried out for the Royal Society of Chemistry and the Council for Industry and Higher Education found that among the main reasons small employers had not previously offered placements to students were that they had never been approached (Mason, 1996).

> Perhaps there needs to be more of a link between the place of study and the work place. Higher Education could organise more work experience for under-graduates. We could take on more sandwich students.
>
> (Research and Information Manager, medium-sized community health authority)

For students, the resource issue is of the funding of higher education, which is expected to have a substantial impact on students. There are concerns that students will be reluctant to pay up to £500 fees to the university for the privilege of spending a year out on a sandwich placement. It has been conjectured that more students will take a break during a conventional three-year degree, to obtain significant work experience, which does not involve them in paying fees, rather than take a sandwich year. The implications of this may be that only those students from privileged backgrounds will be able to afford to do conventional four-year sandwich degrees (Paddon-Smith, 1997).

If being in higher education means running up large debts, students will tend to opt for a sandwich year if it pays more than it costs and also if they are convinced that the experience will help them gain a job in the future. Both of these are gambles that students may be unwilling to take.

Students eager to find work experience are vulnerable to exploitation, particularly if the student arranges their own placement. One of the benefits of the sandwich scheme is that, if the scheme is well supported by the university, there should be built-in processes that protect students from exploitation by employers.

> In the main, I suppose the average overall would be £10K–£10.5K, but there are people who are earning less than that as well, and we do get one or two placement opportunities coming up where I basically make a decision that they are trying to exploit the student and I never advertise them, because they just want slave labour. I am not prepared to put people into a situation where they are exploited.   (Thorn, 1997)

Some students who undertake placements receive no payment at all other than a grant or bursary that is administered by the university. Placements linked to professional courses are mostly unpaid although students are eligible to receive a grant while they undertake their placement. This is more likely to occur in the public sector and particularly under Schedule 5 of the LEA grant regulations (which will disappear with the ending of the maintenance grant). Similarly, students on short embedded work experience are unlikely to get paid. As a result, many students experience considerable financial hardship especially when they may incur extra expenses for travelling and subsistence. Problems with grant entitlement may also occur when students combine an unpaid placement with paid part-time work, although this will no longer be a problem with the ending of the maintenance grant.[2]

There is some uncertainty about the demand for, and future funding of, sandwich degrees and thus concern that the four-year sandwich degree will disappear, especially where it involves an unpaid placement. Some higher education institutions, in particular, have built a reputation around the provision of vocational courses:

> Some students come to Middlesex because of the placement. In light of the reforms to funding, we are currently reviewing our placement options and considering alternatives to the traditional sandwich placement so that students will continue to choose Middlesex University.
>
> (Paddon-Smith, 1997)

In anticipation, some universities are cutting the four-year sandwich courses to three years while trying to maintain the maximum work experience element without compromising the quality of the 'service' to employers or the learning experience of the student.

> There are marketing advantages to shortening courses... losing a year without compromising the quality... the trick is to include a work placement element without lengthening the course... where a placement is not essential to the learning experience on the course, there is a temptation to get out of them. Placements are a nuisance to find, and monitor. They have huge advantages if done properly, otherwise there is not a lot to be said for maintaining them.
>
> (Walkling, 1996)

Organisation

One of the biggest barriers to expansion is that employers schedules do not fit in to the academic timetable. Year-long placements are often geared to being between October and June and shorter placements usually have to fit in to academic terms or semesters. This does not necessarily coincide with the requirements of employers.

> A major problem for academics is the written work that accompanies the placement which has to be collected in and marked before the student can progress to the next year. If the student does that placement very late, they may miss this deadline. The course is flexible enough to accommodate a special extension in a one-off situation but not if 40 or 50 students require this.
>
> (Spencer, 1997)

Although the four-year sandwich course is seen by employers, students and many academics as an 'ideal' model, its relative inflexibility can be a problem. There are a number of alternative ways of embedding work-experience opportunities within courses. Many such programmes provide undergraduates with the opportunity to undertake shorter periods of work experience, usually relevant to their discipline. The ways in which work-experience opportunities are organised and the role of higher education staff involved in the process are critical factors.

---

2   Funding arrangements, of course, are set to change in the next academic year. For example, on nursing degrees, where the clinical placement is a major element of the education, students are paid a bursary. However, from 1998/99, the Department of Health will fully fund new students on nursing and midwifery degrees and certain other health-related professional courses.

There are lessons to be learned from the experiences of various professional placements in terms of the ways in which such courses are structured. Professional placements have a long history of embedding work experience into courses so that students develop into competent professionals by the end of the course. The majority of such programmes involve blocks of work experience balanced with periods of study at university (Appendix 1).

Shorter opportunities can be rewarding and there are many innovative examples of different ways of embedding work-experience opportunities into courses. One such example is an Honours degree in Leisure Management at Manchester Metropolitan that offers a three-year programme combining academic study with professional training in the field through 'applied study periods'. The course is modular with an associated system of credits. Students have the opportunity to gain experience in different sectors of the leisure industry, enabling them to apply their knowledge, develop their skills and observe professionals at work. Other models are organised so that students can do their placement for one day a week if there are no classes.

Short, unpaid, work experience needs careful monitoring to avoid exploitation. For example, the Producers Alliance for Cinema and Television (PACT) have a Voluntary Code of Practice which has grown out of concern about exploitative practices in the industry's increasingly-fragmented labour market. The code embodies six basic principles including recommendations about companies offering unpaid work experience for students on formal educational courses. According to the code, companies should provide practical work experience, offer a written report to their academic supervisors and cover all reasonable out-of-pocket expenses. The Code states that 'unpaid work experience should always be very short in duration, no more than four weeks. After this the position should become a paid training post' (PACT, 1996).

Creating Opportunities

The current provision of placements seems to vary depending on the type of placement, the way that they are organised and marketed, and the expectations of students. Some departments, notably those who had a well-resourced placement operation, reported little resistance from employers to provide opportunities for students and a few indicated that they had more place-ment vacancies than students to fill them (Paddon-Smith, 1997).

> One of the things that has cropped up in an awful lot of cases is: 'we are in the process of reorganising, it wouldn't be fair to bring someone in'; or 'we are making redundancies, we can't be seen to be making permanent people redundant and bringing students in at the same time'. That is a totally understandable political thing really. Other than that I have to say I don't find that much resistance.
>
> (Thorn, 1997)

> There is no gap between the supply and demand of placements at least in [Business and Languages]. All those students who want a placement get one. However, allocating enough French work placements can sometimes prove problematic, therefore students are required to have a back-up placement at a French university of their choice in case their work placement preference falls through.
>
> (Baines, 1997)

One source of placements is students who have been through the placement experience and are now employers themselves;

> So students are very pro-placement once they have been through the process. They very often come back to us after graduation, asking 'have you got any students?'. They create new opportunities for us.
>
> (Lee, 1997)

Although it appears that some academics are resistant to the idea of work experience, particu-larly in some subject areas, there is a sense in which the culture of resistance is changing as new staff enter the system, many of whom have come from industry and appreciate the value of work experience (Baines, 1997).

Summary

This chapter has explored the benefits for different stakeholders that are specific to course embedded work experience opportunities and has identified a number of barriers that may impede the expansion of provision.

- The traditional year-long sandwich placement, either for an academic or calendar year, is often viewed as the exemplary form of work placement, combining a long period of immersion in the work-place setting with course relevance and well-developed structures of support and monitoring.

- Employers tend to consider longer rather than shorter periods of placement as more meaningful: six-to-twelve months gives employers time to establish relationships, not just with students but with staff in their academic institutions.

- There are fears among academics that the economic constraints faced by employers reduces the scope for substantial expansion of the one-year placement.

- There are substantial benefits to be gained from embedded work experience despite some initial up-front costs.

- There may be room for expansion of one-year placements, particularly in SMEs who do not have placement students at all, though some form of incentive may be needed to initiate the process.

- Shorter periods of work experience as part of the programme of study can be integrated into courses in a variety of ways and have many associated benefits for employers, students and higher education staff.

- Links with academic institutions through placements enable employers to help promote and reinforce a learning culture.

- Employers who invest in a placement culture stand to gain a healthy return in terms of the enthusiasm and new ideas that students bring with them.

- Although there are many variations in the length, and the ways in which the work experience element is organised, embedded work experience is recognised as a significant channel for student learning. The student learning experience is enhanced through the application of theory and the development of practical skills in a work environment.

- Students develop a range of 'employability' skills while on placement. Graduate recruiters value the placement experience because applicants are better able to articulate and provide evidence of key skills.

- A period of time spent in a workplace setting provides students with a valuable opportunity to explore their suitability for an area of work and to make valuable contacts.

- For a quality experience, it is important that placements of any length are adequately supported academically and administratively by appropriately trained staff. In some places, there is institutional pressure to cut back on the tutoring service, which will have adverse effects on the quality of the experience. It is particularly important that overseas placements are adequately monitored to ensure that maximum benefit accrues from the placement.

- All parties need to have clear learning objectives embodied in a contract so that they all know their responsibilities. It is essential that the students are involved in any negotiations to get some sense of ownership and take responsibility for their own learning.

- The total experience is enhanced if the placement is formally recognised and assessed as part of the degree. Assessments tend to be based on essays written about the placement experience, evaluations of learning logs or projects undertaken during the placement.

- There are concerns that students will be reluctant to pay fees to the university for the privilege of spending a year out on placement. The costs of being in higher education, for many students, may mean running up large debts and this will perhaps deter students from taking the sandwich option.

- Paid placements make a favourable contribution to a student's income. As well as the recognition of work that a salary brings, students appreciate the opportunity of becoming financially independent.

- Students eager to find work experience are vulnerable to exploitation, particularly if the student arranges their own placement. Students who undertake unpaid placements may experience considerable financial hardship especially if they incur extra expenses for travelling and subsistence.

- One of the biggest barriers to expansion is that employers' schedules do not fit in to the academic timetable. Although the four-year sandwich course is seen by employers, students and many academics as an 'ideal' model, its relative inflexibility can be a problem.

- In terms of expansion, the provision of work-experience opportunities varies depending on the type of placement, the way that they are organised and marketed, and the expectations of students. Some departments, notably those who had a well-resourced placement operation, reported little resistance from employers to provide opportunities for students.

4 Project-linked work experience

This chapter explores the benefits and barriers to expansion of project-linked work experience. Where appropriate, examples of good practice are outlined and suggestions made as to how barriers to further expansion may be overcome.

What is project-linked work experience

Project-linked work experience involves one or more undergraduates working for, or with, a company on an employer-generated project. Projects may have been specifically identified and defined with an undergraduate in mind, or may be as a result of an existing company need having been fine-tuned to make it suitable for an undergraduate project.

This is in contrast to a more general work-experience placement where the focus may be on giving the student a fairly rounded experience of the workplace and a taste of the company culture. In a large firm, general work experience might involve an appreciation of the systems that operate at different levels. In a smaller firm, students might have the opportunity to work directly on some or all of the firm's processes. In contrast, project-linked work experience may be confined to a small aspect of the organisation. Therefore, project-linked work experience can be of shorter duration than a more general placement and still be meaningful. The student simply has a discrete 'real world' task to complete.

Course-embedded and extracurricular project-linked work experience

Project-linked work experience can be divided roughly into two categories. It can be course-embedded, forming an integral part of the curriculum and course requirements, or it can be external to the course, being undertaken primarily during vacation periods, typically during the long summer vacation.[1]

Project-linked work experience, embedded in the undergraduate curriculum, tends to receive support and guidance from the university or course team throughout the entire placement process.

Course-embedded projects may involve students working individually or in teams, for example:

- The School of Property and Construction, at UCE, runs an inter-professional project (IPP) where teams of 6–10 students work for a real or simulated client. The project is rated as equivalent to a one-semester module.

- Aston University has an industrial project for full-time, final-year undergraduates, which involves working on problems and projects set by engineers in industry.

- The University of Leeds have developed an initiative (CRISP) to encourage and help local organisations access students' project-based work as part of their course, enabling organisations to benefit from academic expertise. The initiative involves undergraduates and postgraduates from a large number of departments. Projects can last from a few weeks to a year and bring a group of students together to work on a collaborative project crossing various subject areas. The project is supervised by a member of staff whose area of interest and research is related to the project.

---

1 Although some 'brokering' arrangements, such as Business Bridge in Merseyside cut across this distinction, any single project will still fall into one of these two categories.

- 'Live projects' at Napier University involve groups of four students working on projects designed by employers. The projects last 6–8 weeks and the courses involved are Hospitality, Business and Information Management and Computer Studies. The aim of the project is to show students the workplace and enable them to work in teams. The scheme is funded by the Scottish Higher Education Funding Council. There is a liaison person for the University and this is the point of contact for employers. Employers design the projects and they are tailored by academics. The projects must not be essential to the employer, rather they are an educational opportunity for the students. The employer is expected to give 6–8 hours to the project. Evaluation has shown that where students have direct contact with employers their motivation to engage in the tasks will be increased (Stewart & Macleod, 1997).

- Northumbria University arranges paid, project-based, work experience for six months to one year. There are also some shorter projects which are unpaid, and are either one day a week or for a block of time. Most are integral to the course.

- Lancaster University's School of Independent Studies used 'live' team employer-linked projects as part of the first-year experience.

- Portsmouth University has developed a scheme (COHEsion) where students work on specific employer projects for 3–6 months. These are typically technical in nature. Employers are encouraged to offer projects on which a group of students can work. Employers can also access expertise and equipment within the university, and so the selling point to them is that they will be able to undertake a project that might not normally be possible.

- Manchester School of Engineering piloted an approach to establishing and testing a methodology for generating, running and monitoring projects directed at current industrial problems.

The number of institutions of higher education, which have programmes of study that involve students undertaking projects with external organisations, is growing.

Employer-linked projects during the vacation are more likely to have been initiated by individual students. Typically, such projects involve academic staff to a lesser extent, or not at all. Students often receive support from outside agencies, concerned with development, training and enterprise, such as Training and Enterprise Councils (TECs), Local Enterprise Councils (LECs) and Business Links.

Examples of project-linked work-experience schemes using brokering agencies include:

- STEP, a national programme sponsored by Shell that runs eight-week project placements in SMEs.

- Business Bridge, a scheme run by three universities in Merseyside. They offer a flexible approach to placing students in SMEs to carry out projects, which could be for either course-embedded projects or extracurricular schemes or both. (They also provide 'bridges' for traditional placements and part-time paid work).

- Profit by Placement, a scheme run through the Glasgow Development Agency, which has good links with SMEs due to its business training, start-up grants and marketing-support role.

- A range of projects in the East Midlands, established under the Higher Education Regional Development Fund, that are attempting to provide project-linked experiences for students in SMEs.

The benefits of project-linked work experience

Benefits to employers

Employers of all sizes can benefit from providing project-linked opportunities for single students or teams of students. Host firms can have specialised projects completed, at a fraction of the cost of employing consultants.[2] Depending upon the particular scheme, firms may receive help from local agencies in identifying and defining a project that would bring significant improvements to the business.

Alternatively, project-linked work experience could provide a firm with a way of getting a project completed that would otherwise, because of a lack of time or resources, never get off the ground. Through employing a student, or team of students to work on the project, companies have the chance to utilise the skills, knowledge and technological expertise of undergraduates. Students may bring a fresh approach to the company; sometimes acting as agents of change.

Project-linked schemes can also give firms the opportunity to forge links with specialist departments in their local universities to provide the foundation for mutually productive partnerships in the future, in which expertise and resources might be shared. They may also give the opportunity to develop links with local agencies, such as TECs.

Although the main purpose is to develop a specific project, this type of work experience might also be used as a recruitment tool, or trial experience for employers who do not have a history of recruiting graduates.

> We take a small number of students in their final summer vacation who come in and work on a specific project for six or seven weeks. It works quite well, firstly because it is giving a student an insight into what it is like working here but second it is giving us a chance to look at them in case they want to apply for a job here. That's the benefit.
>
> (Manager, large public financial institution)

> We provide work experience, we provide projects to the undergraduates so that we are sucking them into the organisation. We are getting them to know us, so that when they have finished their degree they don't even worry about a job, they don't even worry about the fact that we are not the world's best payers, they know we have got some exciting projects, because they have been in, they have been involved in it and they will happily come along to us.
>
> (Senior Manager, large manufacturing organisation)

It might also be used as a stepping-stone to the provision of more extensive work-experience opportunities. Some schemes, for example, offer cash benefits for businesses willing to provide opportunities and can provide SMEs with a low-commitment method of exploring the area of work-experience than would be required by taking on a student for a longer period of time. One of the aims of STEP, for example, is to demonstrate the benefits of recruiting graduates to small firms. The STEP project has benefited two thirds of the companies involved by increasing efficiency, bringing technology to the business and introducing new and improved marketing practices. STEP also aims to develop small business capability and help SMEs realise the longer-term benefits of employing undergraduates. In addition, the STEP annual regional and national competitions provide good publicity for the participating SMEs.

Centering the experience around a specific and achievable project means that work experience has clear boundaries and there is less onus on the employer to provide a 'rounded' experience of all aspects of the organisation.

Benefits to students

Project-linked work experience gives students the opportunity to apply their knowledge in a practical, focused way.

> We offer an undergraduate vocational training scheme. In their last year of study they can take six weeks out and do a project with us so they get a physical chance of working in a store. They tend to work in several different departments and then they get projects set either by the branch manager or their institution.
>
> (Deputy Store Manager, large retail company)

---

2   A note of caution should be expanded where project-linked work experience students are perceived to be in direct competition with emerging companies or consultants working in the field already. There is the possibility that companies will complain to their employer networks and organisations if unqualified students are undercutting them. Potentially, this could result in action being taken against a course or institution. Some courses have avoided this potential problem by using simulated projects, or concentrating on projects that are not essential to the organisation.

Project-linked work experience provides the opportunity to develop an array of employability skills. However, the main skills developed by project-linked work experience are problem solving, time management, organisation and general awareness of the time-frame in which employer organisations operate.

> They get some understanding of what's different about working for a company. Everything is different... this is like doing academic work but with the additional strain of everything mattering. You are working on it, there's a report, there's a well to be drilled. Things are happening. You come in and you do a job and it really makes a difference. It isn't marked, its tested, and that's different. They start understanding what makes business in general tick.
>
> (Strategic Manager, multi-national petro-chemical company)

In some circumstances the involvement in employer-linked projects allowed undergraduates to demonstrate their potential for working in the small business sector, in addition to the larger firms that have traditionally provided work-experience opportunities. Schemes such as 'STEP into the Community'[3] also widen opportunities to work in the not-for-profit sector.

Non-course-embedded, vacation project-linked work experience also allows students to earn money whilst undertaking work likely to enhance their curriculum vitae. On programmes, such as STEP and Profit by Placement, students are given an allowance by the company for whom they work. Furthermore, project work may lead to further work experience opportunities. Indeed, in 1997, for example, 44% of STEP students were offered further work, up 4% on the previous year (Cullen, 1998).

Some non-course embedded schemes provide students with support in reflecting on and articulating their experiences.

Benefits to staff in higher education institutions

The main benefit of project-linked work experience for academics is that it provides an opportunity for students to apply specific skills or knowledge in a tightly constrained setting. Rather than a more general experience, on a year placement, for example, where students develop a highly variable set of skills and abilities, the embedded project approach enables academics to monitor more closely the specific progress of the work experience.

Furthermore, the specific project setting enables students to reflect directly on success and failure in completing tasks, on barriers to undertaking the project and how they were overcome, and in determining precisely what skills and abilities were developed as part of the process.

The 'learning contract' between the institution, employer and student can be tightly specified and the obligations of all parties clear. For some academics, this clear specification of project-linked experience makes it easier to 'sell' the idea of work-experience to employers as it involves less commitment than the longer periods of work placement (Chapter 3).

Where the project experience is outside the programme of study, academics benefit by having the laborious work of finding and organising work experience taken 'off their hands'.

Some academics have reservations about externally organised project-based work experience because they want it to be linked to the programme of study, either because they want to see particular subject matter put into practice or because they consider employability skills as intrinsic to the higher education experience. Where project-linked work experience is embedded in the programme of study, higher education staff may make use of brokering agencies (such as Business Bridge) to help establish project links, but more often have to find, or assist students in their search for, appropriate projects.

Project-linked work experience has also provided a way to begin to build partnerships between higher education institutions and SMEs as it may, for example, point to potential areas of research collaboration and consultancy.

---

3   'STEP into the Community' has been running since 1993 and offers the voluntary sector a resource for the development and implementation of specific projects to improve efficiency and boost fund-raising opportunities.

Meaningful and intended experience

Project-linked work experience is generally perceived as being 'meaningful' for students. Employers perceive project working, whether by individual students or by a team of students, as providing a taster of 'real world' problem solving and as developing some appreciation of commercial time frames.

Students tend to appreciate that project-based work provides them with a focus for developing subject-related skills and for applying knowledge. This is a view endorsed by academic teaching staff, especially where the project is an embedded part of the programme of study. In some cases it also provides an opportunity to work in a 'realistic' team setting. Project work is meaningful, not in terms of the project itself, but in terms of the learning that comes from undertaking the project.

> In the first term of the final year there is an integrated project as well, where you work with estate managers, architects and town planners and you have a problem that you have to resolve and you have to work together to resolve the problem. There is an actual report and when you present the report it is to people outside the college who are involved in industry, and to local authorities who are actually dealing with the scheme outside of the college. It was a real scheme, not a mock-up. We worked at Newtown – it was City Challenge – and we had to put a document together on how to improve the area, including what sort of shops are required, what the community wanted, just a general enhancement.
>
> (Recent graduate, small quantity surveyors)

However, employers, students and academic staff are aware that some project-based working can be artificial, in as much as the project has been created or organised in a way that is external to the everyday functioning and priorities of the employer.

> It did offer work placement and live projects but the live projects weren't really like projects, if it had been a true live project we would have a couple of days to do something instead we had a few weeks, which you don't get in business.   (Studio Manager, small design and print agency)

There may also be a tendency for some employers, especially in larger organisations, to view the time-frame in which most projects are undertaken as too short to appreciate fully the nature of working within an organisation. Similarly, some students also feel that project-linked work experience allows them to only 'scratch the surface' of an organisation. However, students may benefit from undertaking a range of projects throughout their degree and transferring the learning from one setting to another.

There is also the issue, especially for staff in higher education institutions, as to whether project-based work experience, which is part of the programme of study, actually links to the objectives of the course in practice. It seems, although evidence is anecdotal, that as programme objectives become more closely specified, employer-linked project work is related closely to clearly defined outcomes.

Reflection

Intention and reflection are key to capturing the learning associated with work experience (Chapter 2). This reflection has been given a structure in many project-linked placements, which require students to make a record of, and be explicit about, the skills they have developed as a result of undertaking the work. For example, a student on a STEP-based computer-programming project noted that:

> My main area of improvement has been in communicating and presenting information. This has been mainly due to the training day but also as a result of the demonstrations of software to the customers. I have also improved greatly in self-management. I have been working by myself frequently, managing my own time, and I have developed this skill significantly.

Similarly, a student engaged on a geology and applied geotechnology project reflected upon the improvement in his communication skills as a result of the tasks he had undertaken during the placement:

> Initially I felt less confident about communicating and presenting information, working in teams and self confidence and personal drive. After doing the STEP scheme I feel more confident about my skills in general. I have gained experience of working in teams and presenting information to someone or a group of people and generally improved my overall skill level.

Many project-linked placements and schemes require students to keep a journal or diary of significant events while they are working on their project, or write a report about the project on its completion. If their potential is utilised these reports or journals can form a 'learning log' for the students, which help them to reflect upon their own learning. They enable students to learn *how* they learn, which promotes ownership of, and responsibility for, their own learning. Support in writing these learning logs also enables students to articulate their learning in forms that are accessible to both academics and employers.

It is important that the learning developed during work experience is contextualised within the student's whole experience of learning. The STEP *Skills Tracker* encourages students to place the learning on the STEP scheme in the wider context of their pre-existing abilities. The STEP *Skills Tracker* CD-ROM is a model of good practice in encouraging students to reflect on their own learning. It encourages students to break down their total experience and reflect on different key skills separately during each week of their eight-week project placement. The *Skills Tracker* contains a 'Skills Review' in the form of a log book. It prompts students to document their experiences in, and reflect upon: working in teams, communicating and presenting information, focusing on results, information search skills, demonstrating self-confidence and personal drive and self-management. The *Skills Tracker* helps students think about the skills they already had but were perhaps unaware of:

> I have developed confidence in my ability to complete tasks in the workplace and communicate with others. At the start I was very unsure of what I was capable of. I have now had an opportunity to show others as well as myself that I can work competently from my own initiative.

The reflective process can also promote better utilisation of existing skills, together with an awareness of skills that are particularly important to a conducive working environment. For example, the inter-professional project at UCE requires students to produce a report that includes their observations of the dynamics within their team and relate this to theoretical explanations of teamwork and team development.

Furthermore, the resulting self-awareness of how best to learn can be used to improve learning effectiveness in the future: a vital tool if undergraduates are to become lifelong learners.

> My information search skills have certainly improved. I have learnt to ask the right questions and research my work thoroughly. Focusing on my objectives have made me work more efficiently and effectively.

A key factor in the process of reflection is that reports should not simply be a list of what happened during the project. They should also include the students' own reflections and feelings about the project work that they undertook. This could include documenting the positive and negative aspects of the project and critically analysing the ways in which problems were solved or might have been solved.

Quality

It is important to the undergraduate, the employer, the higher education institution or broker agency that, in addition to the successful completion of the project, the work experience is of a high quality. Ideally, the responsibility to ensure that quality is maintained and monitored would lie jointly with the employer and the higher education institution or agency. In practice, the extent to which the employer becomes actively involved in aspects of quality monitoring may vary depending on the degree to which the employer 'owns' the work experience process.

One way to ensure and enhance the quality of project-linked work experience is to adopt a rigorous selection procedure when identifying suitable students for projects. This not only, potentially, matches students to projects but ensures that employers have produced detailed project plans and specified an achievable project. This helps to ensure that projects are applicable to the programme of study or to the externally-brokered scheme. However, there is an issue as to who should take responsibility for selection.

Familiarisation and briefing

All parties involved in the work experience process (student, employer, agency, higher education institution staff) should undergo some form of briefing prior to the start of the project itself. Through initial familiarisation, the project aims can be clarified and a rapport can begin to develop between those involved.

There are other issues that need to be addressed by student, employer, academic staff and broker to ensure the quality of the project-based experience. These include monitoring the relevance of the project, assessing the length and time involved, the viability of the proposal, and agreeing funding, salary or expenses.

Academic staff and brokers need to ensure that appropriate health and safety, insurance and equal opportunities procedures are in place, to make arrangements for regular visits and to make sure supervisory staff are adequately trained. Students need to monitor and reflect on their learning in order to get as much out of the project as possible.

Where project-linked, work-experience schemes are preceded by a training or orientation programme, participating students also benefit from this extra induction measure. Although the nature of induction programmes varies between schemes and institutions, they can benefit students who attend them in two ways. First, they prepare students for their work experience and can play an important part in managing students' expectations. Ensuring that student are clear about what to expect during their project can play a crucial role in determining that their experience is a success. Second, they provide a foundation of knowledge and skills that may be applied in a variety of situations, not just during a short period of project-linked work experience. Examples of orientation programmes include Profit by Placement's business skills training week, the STEP induction programme as well as various schemes run by large employers:

> We take a number of students on a scheme that is called Horizon, which is timed between school and university, so 18 year olds. They are with us for 8 months and then they go on travels before they go to university. The one that is coming to me will be working on a specific project that I am working on and will be treated like one of us. I did it, actually, and it was immensely valuable. I had a wonderful time. I would recommend it to anybody as long as they are going to an organisation that does have a *proper* programme. They come in and have a couple of weeks training, then work from October through until Christmas, then another week's training, and then back on the project until about June.
>
> (Manager, large management consultants)

Ongoing monitoring and supporting ongoing reflection

Progress should be monitored at regular intervals throughout the life of the project, perhaps through visits and meetings between key personnel such as the student, the employer or supervisor, the student's academic tutor, or a representative from the relevant broker agency.

Visits and meetings are vital to identify any problems that are occurring, so that steps can be quickly taken to address these. By identifying and solving problems as they occur, potential project failures can be avoided. It is vital that there are mechanisms in place to try to overcome problems as they arise, to salvage individual projects and to protect the reputation of the scheme, higher education institution, or employer. Failure to do this could result in a refusal by parties who have been dissatisfied, as a result of adverse experiences in the past, to participate in similar collaborations in the future.

Students may also play a part in monitoring and maintaining the quality of project-linked work experience, through the reports that they are normally required to produce. Reports, which include elements of students' reflections on their learning during the project, have the potential to provide employers and higher education institutions with indicators of what constitutes a successful, high-quality placement.

Debriefing

Debriefing is an important area of project work, irrespective of whether the project is completed successfully or not. Not only is it important to discuss how the project succeeded or failed, it is important to discuss the mode and style of working, interpersonal relations, teamworking (where relevant) and communication issues. Debriefing helps complete the reflection cycle (Chapter 2). Debriefing is probably the least developed quality element in most project-linked work experience. Standardised feedback devices, such as the STEP exit survey of employers and students, may stand in lieu of detailed, direct project debriefing.

Assessment and accreditation of project-linked work experience

Where project-linked work experience is an embedded part of the academic course, it is often assessed towards the programme award. Assessment takes place for two reasons.

First, if it is not assessed then it is not usually given credit towards the programme of study. Where a work-linked project is all or part of a module of study, then it needs to be assessed in a manner consistent with assessment on other modules.

Second, assessment helps students to value the opportunity. If the embedded work-linked project is not assessed it is less likely to be taken seriously by students, or at the very least, not likely to be given priority when other assessed work is pressing. Furthermore, if the work-linked project is an optional element, students are unlikely to choose it if they get no credit for the work.[4]

There are issues of what is actually assessed in such circumstances. On one hand, a student, or group of students, has undertaken to complete a project and so it might be expected that the assessment focuses on the extent to which the project has been successful. On the other hand, the project is a vehicle for the development of a range of employability skills and it may be appropriate to assess such skills' development. In practice, the higher education institution assesses the final output of the project, often in written form. This may be the project, *per se*, as undertaken for the employer or it may be, or include, a critical review and analysis of the project process, an exploration of issues that arise, or some other form of written account of outcome, even when the outcome, for the employer, is a failure.

For example, a project may involve the setting up of a client database. The academic supervisor may not assess that outcome as such, as it may be difficult to fine-grade the product or to provide evidence to external examiners. Instead, the assessment may be based on a written account of the process and a critical review of the issues, irrespective of whether or not the database works to specification.

---

4   It needs to be stressed that employers value work experience, irrespective of whether it is assessed or not. The onus is on students to articulate its value to them personally and then to relate it to employers' needs when they make their applications.

In addition to credit towards the programme award, embedded project-linked work experience may also attract other forms of accreditation. This may be in the form of external body recognition and certification of the successful completion of the project, including recognition by any brokering agency involved in arranging the work experience, or additional certification on the part of the higher education institution. At the very least, additional credit may be given to the work through testimonials provided by the employer or the student supervisor.

Extracurricular, project-linked work experience is much less likely to be assessed towards a programme award because it tends to be far more difficult for academic staff to monitor and undertake meaningful assessment. Brokering agencies and employers are unlikely to want, or be able, to assess the experience in a way that is consistent with other assessment procedures within the programme of study.

However, it is possible for extracurricular project work to be accredited by the brokering agency or through some external accreditation system. Again, credit may be attributed via testimonials provided by the employer.

Barriers to expansion of project-linked work experience

Resources

Even a relatively short, project-linked placement may prove to be prohibitive to a small employer in terms of cost. In addition to the organisation paying the student an allowance, if required, there are additional costs in terms of staff time.

Host employers have also to invest a certain amount of up-front time to identify and define a project. They also need to provide students with adequate induction procedures including health and safety instruction. In addition, there is ongoing support for, and supervision of, the student(s) undertaking the project and this requires allowing other employees to take time out from their usual duties.

The commitment that is required from companies to get involved with providing work experience for undergraduates may be too great, when they cannot immediately see the benefits they will reap.

Such resource concerns, especially among SMEs, may be assuaged to some extent by the use of short-term subsidies. Subsidies may provide sufficient incentive to encourage involvement and, once convinced of the benefits, subsidised employers may be willing to make more of a financial investment in the future.

Programmes such as STEP and Profit by Placement subsidise the payment to students, thus making the schemes attractive to SMEs. However, large-scale development of such schemes would clearly raise questions about the source of subsidies. The government may need to contribute more, for example, through development agencies or the number of private-sector contributors would need to be expanded.

If the project is for an employer but carried out whilst the student or team is still based at the university or higher education institution, then the employer would probably need to devote time to visiting the university department to oversee the project at intervals. Some companies, particularly SMEs, may not traditionally have worked in a way that would allow time to be spent away from the organisation for such purposes, or may be reluctant or unable to offer enough supervision.

In the case of a relatively new scheme like *Profit by Placement*, some firms are currently unable to participate since they have not had time to adequately define a project. Without a tightly-defined project plan, they are unable to take advantage of the opportunity to have a student working on a project for them. However, with adequate support from development agencies, this time constraint will hopefully rectify itself.

Time and commitment issues are exacerbated if a placement does not go well. Companies are more likely to lose interest in the scheme than try to look at what went wrong and find ways to overcome problems in the future. Problems usually occur when the definition of the programme and the outcomes are unclear, or if the student is not given enough time. Problems can also arise when the company and the student are not a good match.

The likelihood of a project going badly can be minimised by the quality monitoring processes already outlined including the rigorous definition of a project, the careful selection and training of undergraduates, and by monitoring the progress of the student(s) and the project, together with the host employer's perceptions throughout the project duration. Such an approach may appear to prohibit the numbers of project-linked work-experience schemes that could take place, but it ensures that once an employer has been persuaded to join the scheme their interest is not lost through a bad experience that could have been prevented.

Glasgow's 'Profit by Placement' scheme provides an example of this approach. It concentrates on making a small number of project-linked opportunities extremely effective for both student and employer and takes the view that this will ensure the continuation and expansion of the scheme in the long term.

The main barrier preventing the expansion of placement agencies such as the STEP scheme is money, which dictates how many placements can be organised and funded. In 1997, students were paid an allowance of £100 a week. There are local sponsors who contribute to costs, although the host companies pay between 50–75% of the student's training allowance. The balance between host and sponsor varies from locality to locality. In addition to paying an allowance, a large amount of administrative support is needed to maintain the quality of the scheme.

Funding may also be a barrier to agencies supporting the students' reflection on the learning. For example the funding of Business Bridge dictates the output, that is that they have a target of 1100 SMEs on board by Spring 1999. So their core function is based on the improvement of businesses and they currently do not have enough funding to concentrate on supporting student learning.

Project-linked schemes need to be sold to the business development network or local development company network as a simple and cost-effective way of developing their companies. If projects are sold as being useful to companies and those that become involved are convinced of the benefits, then this can create an active demand from companies of all sizes for undergraduates to work on projects for them and problems of time and commitment could be minimised. Expansion of project-linked schemes does not necessarily impact negatively on quality, indeed, expansion could help to improve the quality as schemes gain more experience and expertise, allowing them to become more finely tuned.

Organisation

Project-linked, work-experience schemes, which have been working well in Britain, focus around creating a *demand from firms* for undergraduate students to work on projects for them. Thus, to enable firms to recognise the potential benefits of providing project-linked work experience, information about the scheme should be accessible to employers.

Promoting schemes amongst the business and industrial sector helps to raise awareness. This is important in attracting small and medium sized enterprises (SMEs), as they do not traditionally offer opportunities to undergraduates because they are unaware of the benefits to their business. To encourage their participation, there should be help available in the identification of a problem or need which could generate a project. Giving the companies a choice of placement students, together with a clear idea of what they can expect from the student and what is expected from them, can help make the company more eager to participate. Finally, employers should be given the opportunity to feedback on their experience to help to improve the process in the future.

As project-based work experience tends to be of shorter duration than traditional sandwich-year placements, there is a need for the students to make the most of it from the outset. This requires effective organisation, with importance placed on pre-placement briefing, addressing criteria and goals, and debriefing. Organising work experience within the tight structure, which is needed to monitor each project effectively, requires considerable time, expertise and resources and this too is a barrier to expansion of the project.

Rather than employers offering opportunities to students and universities, the responsibility for finding suitable firms and helping them to identify and define suitable projects could lie with the higher education institutions. This role may be taken on by a broker agency but this is unusual unless the work experience is part of a programme or scheme external to the course.

Creating Opportunities
Information
There is currently a lack of employer awareness of the opportunities that are available to them for bringing undergraduates into firms to work on specific projects. This is particularly acute in the SME sector, where firms tend to consider themselves too small to be suitable, or unable to pay high enough wages to the students who would work for them. There is a latent demand amongst SMEs in the provision of project-linked work experience. SMEs do not currently know enough about the opportunities; what is available and how it could benefit them (Durkan, 1997).

It is important that students are also made aware of the extracurricular opportunities for project-linked work experience that exist for them. To a certain extent this is the responsibility of each individual. However, it is important that information is freely promoted to students in all types of higher education institutions. Students must be educated about what project-linked work experience is, what will be required of them, and how they would benefit. Students are often badly informed about opportunities with SMEs. Furthermore, they often favour 'traditional' forms of work experience, which tend to involve working with larger organisations rather than SMEs. Business Bridge, for example, perceive a cultural gap between SMEs and students that needs to be overcome in order to develop project opportunities of mutual benefit.

For example, there have been national incentives to market the STEP programme to students. Local agents have been working to make careers services aware of the programme. Some agencies have secured the agreement of local education authorities to enclose publicity leaflets with grant cheques. However, the imminent abolition of grants will curtail this approach in the future.

As SMEs are the major source of potential providers of project-linked work experience, they need to be made aware of the possibilities for involvement. More importantly, they need to be alerted to how providing these opportunities will help their businesses. Many SMEs are 'added-value' firms (Appendix 2, Figure A2.3) and they need to be assured that their involvement will be a good investment of their time and money, and that a return is likely.

Some agencies have encountered difficulties in both contacting SMEs, and retaining their interest in providing work-experience opportunities (Wickenden, 1997). If higher education institutions hope to encourage SMEs to offer project-linked experience then they will need to make considerable efforts to forge, and maintain, links with small businesses. Making these links is problematic as SMEs may not operate in a way to allow medium- to long-term strategic planning, often being too involved in the day-to-day problems and running of the business.

A study aimed at SMEs in the West Midlands region found that mailshots were not an effective way of gaining attention – they got lost or ignored amongst all the other paper that SMEs regularly receive about grants and business opportunities. Methods of contact must be very simple, and they should basically be a targeted sales pitch to grab and keep the attention of SMEs. When companies are approached, it is not effective to ask if they want to provide a work experience opportunity for an undergraduate. A positive response would be more likely if companies were asked if they would like an undergraduate to come in and work on a specific project, and then be provided with examples.

Profit through People has tried to overcome SMEs' lack of awareness of opportunities, and generate a higher level of interest, through the circulation of STEP publicity to local SMEs.

The initial attempt to do this was not altogether successful and, as part of the refinement plan, they aim to link up with Graduate Link Birmingham.

An effective approach is likely to be one that points out clearly how the company could benefit from a work-experience project. This could be done through a central co-ordinating body, responsible for researching work-experience opportunities, within the university.

A central work experience agency within a university has the advantage of providing a single point of contact for any employer interested in developing links with higher education. It also serves as a central resource for the university. The disadvantage of this approach is that the common interest in a particular field and the rapport which this can help to develop, is lost through having a more general contact point.

Conversely, staff at the faculty or programme level might forge the links. Although, possibly less efficient and initially more confusing for employers (because of the lack of a 'one-stop' contact point), operating at the programme level can have the advantage of shared language between the academic specialist and the employer, where the proposed project is linked closely to a particular discipline. A shared language may increase the possibility of being able to 'market' project-linked work experience opportunities in a way which is relevant and meaningful to SMEs.

To do this requires innovative course staff who are continually networking and looking out for new opportunities. Networking between firms within a particular sector may also be easier if it is co-ordinated by academics who are specialists in an appropriate field. A good relationship between course staff and local industry should make it much easier to persuade local companies to provide opportunities.

Work experience projects could also be organised through a co-ordinating body for a number of universities in the region, for example Business Bridge co-ordinates projects for three Merseyside universities, Graduates for Greater Manchester aims to co-ordinate work experience for higher education institutions in the region. Alternatively, universities could strengthen this approach by utilising a network of local agencies, government agencies and business organisations.

A co-ordinated approach between universities and outside 'broker' agencies can be used to plug into existing employer networks, overcome apprehension, and relate to companies on their own terms. Using outside agencies as mediators between SMEs and higher education institutions can help to give SMEs a greater feeling of control, making their continued involvement more likely. Agencies can also bridge the conceptual gaps (real or imagined) which may exist between SMEs and higher education institutions, by relating to SMEs in a business-orientated way, rather than in academic terms. Broker agencies can help firms to define specific projects and draw up detailed business development specifications, making the benefits attainable by host employers immediately apparent. This agency intervention at the awareness and project-definition stage is also fundamental in creating the demand from SMEs for placement students.

Policy within higher education institutions

A barrier to obtaining more project-linked work experience opportunities is created by a mis-match between when companies would be willing to provide projects, and when students are available to work on them. In the case of course-embedded projects, this mismatch often arises because of a lack of flexibility within individual course timetables. Companies may not be able to provide projects for students to work upon at the times they would fit into the course structure during the academic year. Project-linked work experience, which is external to the course, usually takes place during the summer vacation, and this too may be an inconvenient time for companies to house or support an undergraduate, since it is the main holiday period for employers as well as students.

Although this suggests a need for more flexibility in course structure, this is far from easy to achieve. It has started to happen in the three Glasgow universities to enable them to take advantage of the term-time opportunities being offered and facilitated by Profit by Placement.

For example, the winter projects can be of variable length and there is no fixed start time. The universities are currently designing courses that would allow more flexible options to accommodate this. However, this can take considerable time; years rather than months, especially in the more traditional universities that do not typically have much work-experience activity.

Summary

- Project-linked work experience (PLWE) involves one or more undergraduates working for, or with, a company on an employer-generated project. Projects may be course-embedded or external to the course, undertaken primarily during the summer vacation.

- Benefits to *employers* of PLWE include getting specialised projects completed at low cost, an opportunity for projects to be undertaken, which otherwise would have remained untouched, and an injection of new ideas in a particular area of concern.

- PLWE also provides employers with a low-risk introduction to the benefits of students and graduates, which may lead to offering further forms of work experience or graduate opportunities. They can also use project-working effectiveness as a means to assess potential recruits.

- Benefits for *students* of PLWE include the opportunity to apply their knowledge in a focused way, whilst developing particular employability skills such as problem solving, time management and organisational abilities.

- PLWE also often provides an opportunity to work in the small-business sector or non-profit making sector, which they may not have otherwise experienced.

- Project working may also lead to further work experience or graduate employment with the organisation.

- PLWE does not add an extra year and it may be easier to fit in with other commitments than, for example, a period of course-embedded work experience.

- For *staff in higher education institutions*, PLWE provides an easier monitoring task, as the project is tightly constrained, compared to more general periods of student 'placement'. There is also the possibility that external brokers relieve some of the problems of identifying work-experience opportunities.

- It is also easier for staff to 'sell' the idea of work experience to organisations because it can be shown to be a relatively low-investment form of work experience.

- PLWE also helps staff in higher education institutions build links with SMEs.

- Project-linked work experience is generally perceived as a *meaningful* experience by employers and students because it provides a taster of 'real world' problem solving.

- Many project-linked placements provide a structure for *reflection* and require students to make a record of, and be explicit about, the skills they have developed as a result of undertaking the project.

- It is important that the work experience is of a high *quality*. Ideally, the responsibility to ensure that quality is maintained and monitored would lie jointly with the employer and the higher education institution or placement agency. It is important that students are matched to projects and that employers have produced detailed specifications for an achievable project, which is regularly monitored.

- Where project-linked work experience is an embedded part of the academic course, it is often *assessed* towards the programme award through the requirement for students to produce a critical review and analysis of the project process.

- Barriers to expansion of project-linked work experience include *resources*. Even a relatively short, project-linked placement may be too much of a resource burden for SMEs, both in terms of up-front costs and staff time. Resource concerns could be offset by the judicious use of short-term subsidies, which may provide initial incentives to become involved.

- Organising work experience, within the tight structure that is needed to monitor each project effectively, requires considerable *time* and expertise and this too is a barrier to expansion of the project.

- Measures to encourage employer participation include: selling the idea as a simple and cost-effective way of developing their companies; making help available in the identification of a problem or need which could generate a project; giving companies a choice of placement students, together with a clear idea of what they can expect from the student; providing a clear statement about what is expected from employers; providing an opportunity for employers to feedback on their experience to help to improve the process in the future.

- Timing of projects is a further barrier: there is often a mismatch between when companies would be willing to provide projects, and when students are available to work on them. In the case of course-embedded projects, this mismatch often arises because of a lack of flexibility within individual course timetables.

5 Term-time, part-time and vacation work

Maximising learning from term-time part-time (TTPT) and vacation work, requires a recognition that learning takes place in a wide variety of situations and settings (Chapter 2). Therefore, learning cannot only be associated with activities that take place within a higher education institution or through work experience that is part of the programme of study. Learning can be part of the work that full-time students undertake during term time and during the vacations (Here we are talking about what could be termed 'traditional' vacation work, that is not work which is project-based or a summer placement.) This type of work can be split into two main categories: paid and voluntary. Many more students are involved in paid work than voluntary work, but most of the initiatives that accredit part-time work are linked to voluntary activities (for example, student tutoring).

Paid work

Full-time students working term-time part-time (TTPT) and in the vacations during their degree is not a new phenomenon. However, changes made to the student funding mechanism over the last decade have resulted in an increase in the number of students needing to undertake paid employment. Radical reforms, including the abolition of state benefits and the reduction in the maintenance grant, have meant the amount of government financial support available to students has substantially decreased. As a result, student hardship has increased, a situation that is set to worsen if post-Dearing speculation regarding the introduction of tuition fees and the abolition of the maintenance grant becomes the reality, and all those families with incomes that exceed £16,000 are forced to make a contribution.

Evidence (CSU-AGCAS-IER, 1996) suggests that students are finding themselves in ever-increasing debt and that many now resort to paid TTPT work for additional income. Estimates of the actual number of students working during term-time vary considerably. At one end of the spectrum, an estimate at the University College of Ripon and York St John suggests that 90% of full-time students work part-time during term time. At the other, Leicester University report only 18.2% of full-time graduates working during term time. Ford *et al* (1995) estimate that the national average is approximately 30% and recently, it has been suggested that the figure is closer to 50% (Berkeley, 1997), an estimate borne out by respondents to the Rover Group (1998) *Young People Development Survey* (Figure 2.1).

Figure 5.1   Surveys and estimates of the percentage of full-time graduates working part-time

Institution	% working part-time during term-time	Year	Source
University of Westminster	45%	1994	Report by Edmundson & Carpenter
University of Central England	30%	1995	Report by Mason and Harvey
Leicester University	18.2%	1995	Report by Hallowell
Oxford Brookes University	57%	1995	Report by Paton-Saltzberg & Lindsay
University of Huddersfield	40%*	1996	Interview with Barry Lee
Ripon & York St John	90%*	1997	Interview with David Browne
Wolverhampton University	50%*	1997	Interview with Colin Appleby
Rover Group	47%	1998	Young People Development Survey

estimates

Anecdotal evidence suggests that this figure more than doubles when traditional vacation work is also taken into account.

Voluntary work

Students undertaking voluntary work are obviously not driven by financial necessity. The main reasons behind undertaking voluntary work are:

- to pursue a particular interest;

- to help people or to make a contribution to society;

- to develop particular skills and attributes;

- to get some experience or make contacts in an area of potential employment.

Students may get involved in voluntary work through various different agencies including local and national organisations and schemes (some specifically aimed at students), initiatives through their institution or their programme of study, or as a result of their own contacts. Examples of structured programmes include:

- *Community Services Volunteers (CSV) Community Enterprise Schemes within Higher Education:* Enterprise projects have been developed to provide students with the opportunity to apply and develop a full range of skills associated with practical and academic study. Projects are constructed to meet an identifiable need in the community;

- *Student tutoring in schools*: a nation-wide initiative with a number of projects being supported by BP, CSV and also local Training Enterprise Councils (TECs). The aim is to provide pupils with positive role models and to offer students the opportunity to broaden their experience and develop transferable skills through participating in a community service, which would benefit all the participants. Schemes are run through student unions and associations and through programmes of study and enterprise units. Examples include: The Tyneside and Northumberland 'Students into Schools' project; Tayside student tutoring scheme; and similar schemes in individual universities including: Glamorgan, Liverpool, Essex, Portsmouth, Surrey, Warwick, Greenwich, North London and University of Wales (Bangor).

- *Youth for Britain* have compiled a huge database of voluntary work opportunities for young people (see Appendix 1). The database provides the information for opportunities but Youth for Britain are not involved in the actual placement of the student or in any ongoing monitoring.

The lack of available statistics make it difficult to estimate the proportion of students who undertake voluntary work. Just under a fifth of graduates (16%) in the Rover Group (1998) *Young People Development Survey* indicated that they had undertaken voluntary work in a not-for-profit organisation during term-time or in vacations.

The benefits of term-time, part-time and traditional vacation work

Benefits to employers and voluntary organisations

Employers benefit from the TTPT and vacation paid work of students in a variety of ways. First, they have a pool of flexible labour they can call on as required. Students, because of study commitments and the way full-time courses are structured, often have to seek work at less sociable hours (evenings, week-ends), which often coincides with employer requirements, especially in service industries. Furthermore, with more flexible modular arrangements students are able to, and do, create days free from university commitments, which means they can be available for employment at peak times for employers, for example, working Fridays in super-markets. Indeed, many unskilled part-time jobs are permanently filled by students.

Similarly, for voluntary organisations, students represent a valuable pool of volunteers, who may be able to offer more flexible hours than other volunteers. In schemes initiated by the university or programme of study, using student volunteers can also help organisations become aware of what universities and colleges have to offer (Buckingham-Hatfield, nd).

Second, this pool of flexible labour is intelligent, quick to learn and good 'value for money' – even if it is money in kind, such as supervisory time. Furthermore, alert employers and voluntary agencies can identify students' potential and use their skills in areas beyond the scope of the initial post to which they were appointed. For example, students often require relatively little supervision and are able to use their initiative. Anecdotes abound about students being 'left in charge' of areas of work, or otherwise given responsibility way beyond what would normally be expected of their job description.

Third, students working in an organisation also provide a potential recruitment opportunity, especially if they see that the organisation recognises their potential whilst working part-time.

> [Our organisation] has something that you either love or you hate. A lot of the time the university people, who have worked for us part time, will join us when they leave university. Some of them will not join us in training management positions, but in an hourly-paid position, that we call a floor manager, and then will work through. Or they might have become a floor manager whilst they are at university working part time.
>
> (Strategic Manager, international fast-food chain)

Benefits to students

For many students, the primary benefit of paid TTPT and vacation work is the much-needed money they earn whilst undertaking full-time study. However, some students recognise that there are associated benefits to earning while learning. TTPT and vacation work may also be the only way some students are able to undertake learning in the work place. Some students, for financial reasons or other commitments such as family responsibilities, are unable to undertake a full-time work placement as part of their course.

TTPT and vacation work also provides a setting within which students can develop employability skills and which they can use to good effect in recruitment interviews.

This form of work may also lead to other forms of work experience. Someone working part-time may have the contacts and a track record within the organisation that might enable them to arrange longer periods of work-experience, such as course-embedded placements or project work.

> When we recruit we have students come in looking for part-time jobs and some of those stay on and become trainee managers, others go on to different schemes.
>
> (Deputy Store Manager, large retail company)

It may also be an opportunity for those students who have traditionally not undertaken work experience as part of their undergraduate course to gain credit for work experience. Accrediting the part-time and vacation work they already do would be a way round this. If TTPT and vacation work is recognised it also adds to the development of the student as a lifelong learner. It encourages students to recognise and maximise learning in everything they do rather than restricting the notion of learning to particular institutions and particular types of work placements. (Issues of accreditation are discussed in detail below.)

There are also specific benefits associated with the work being undertaken on a voluntary basis, which include:

- the opportunity to undertake rewarding work experience;
- recognition from employers of the contribution made by people undertaking work for the good of others;
- an opportunity to broaden experience;
- in some cases, the development of a range of delicate or specific, client-sensitive interactive skills, including communication, negotiation, understanding, and forming and maintaining relationships in order to cope with unusual client needs (Buckingham-Hatfield, nd).

Benefits to staff in higher education institutions

A benefit, from the point of view of staff in higher education, is that students have already found the work. This saves the institution a lot of money in terms of the cost of identifying suitable placements for the students. In turn, this means that the money saved can be channelled into the development of other areas of the placement process.

Students undertaking TTPT work on a voluntary basis may also provide an opportunity for staff to develop links between the institution and the community.

Meaningful and intended experience

Current perceptions of TTPT and vacation work tend to be that, irrespective of marginal benefits other than income, such work does not constitute a meaningful experience for undergraduates. Furthermore, part-time working during term-time, either by full- or part-time students is rarely seen as part of an *intended* learning experience (Chapter 2). In some areas, such as part-time professional qualifications, the cross-over from programme of study and full-time work setting may be considerable, but most TTPT and vacation work is rarely directly related to the academic setting.

The majority of students undertaking paid work do so to earn money and relatively few, it seems, consider the other potential benefits that may accrue from such work. Similarly students who undertake voluntary work do it out of interest or commitment, rather than in any way seeing it as part of a more general learning experience.

Skills gained while working part-time are rarely recognised or acknowledged by the students involved. Indeed, many students regard working part-time as an entirely negative experience that interferes with their course contact-time, their private study time and their leisure time. A 1995 study at UCE (Mason and Harvey, 1995) found that students who worked part-time were more inclined to consider that it had a negative rather than positive effect upon their academic performance. Furthermore, respondents considered that the more hours worked the more adverse the impact on their programme of study. However, there were a small group of students who regarded working part-time for more than 15 hours per week as having a beneficial impact on their study.

Similar results were reported in a study conducted at Paisley University: 'What seems to be emerging is that there was a [negative] impact for those working more than ten hours a week' (THES 23.1.98). However, the researchers found that a fifth of the students said part-time work actually helped their studies. In neither the UCE nor Paisley study is there any indication of how the part-time work was beneficial for the minority groups.

The main reason given for the 'costs' of working part-time is the encroachment on study time. Two-thirds (65%) of the respondents in a recent survey claimed that there are some costs to working part-time during term-time (CRQ, 1997). More than half (66%) of those students who commented on the negative impact of TTPT work remarked that working was time-consuming and therefore meant that they had 'less time for coursework' and were unable to 'put 100% into their degree'. Two respondents claimed that, because they had less time to study, their academic performance had actually suffered.

This negative view of paid term-time, part-time work tends to be perpetuated by academic staff, albeit sometimes by default rather than by intent. Many academic staff ignore term-time, part-time work and regard it as an unfortunate part of student survival rather than as part of the student experience of learning. Staff in higher education institutions are often unaware of the numbers of students working during term-time, the hours spent on part-time work, the nature of that work, the students' reasons for doing it and, thus, the extent to which it impacts on the total student experience. However, most higher education staff are aware that at least some students undertake paid or voluntary work during term time.

The overwhelming perception appears to be that this necessarily has a negative effect on students' academic performance, particularly in terms of the students' ability to attend regularly and to meet deadlines. Academic staff, therefore, often take a dim view of TTPT work, particularly since they are under increased pressure to maintain high levels of attendance and low drop-out rates.

The attitude of academics towards TTPT work, therefore, does not promote a culture in which students feel able to discuss their job and its potential benefits. To the contrary, students feel obliged to actively disguise the fact that they work for fear of reprisal.

> I think there is no honesty about it [term-time part-time work] because students aren't encouraged to declare it. They are afraid that if they do declare it, it will count against them in some way.
>
> (Jackson, 1997)

It could also be argued that the employers of students are also guilty of, at least implicitly, perpetuating the myth that the kinds of jobs they employ students to do on a part-time basis during term-time do not constitute a meaningful experience, other than financial gain. The majority of these jobs are unskilled and of low status, a fact that is very often reflected and reinforced by the poor terms and conditions that accompany them. This is also often true for the paid work students undertake during vacations.

However, there is evidence to suggest that TTPT work can be meaningful. The Rover Group (1998) *Young People Development Survey*, 1997 (Figure 2.1) shows that nearly two-fifths (38%) of the sample who had undertaken part-time, term-time paid employment regarded it as very useful as work experience and a further two fifths (44%) thought it had been 'fairly useful'. Only 2% thought the experience had been no use at all. Similar responses were given regarding paid vacation work: of those who had undertaken this form of work 31% said it was very useful, 51% thought it was fairly useful, and only 4% saw it as not useful at all.

In research conducted at Queen's University, Belfast, half (52.4%) the sample of students recognised that 'working during their undergraduate years would equip them with skills beneficial for future employment'. When asked to identify these skills most students provided broad-based responses alluding to general work experience and effective time management. However, a minority of students referred to the 'key skills identified by employers as the crucial qualities they are looking for in graduates', such as the ability to communicate, to take the initiative and to work in a team (Leonard, 1994, p. 20).

Research conducted in the United States also suggests that 'part-time jobs, especially high quality part-time jobs, may contribute to the career development of the college student' (Kane *et al.*, 1992, p. 138). In addition to gaining skills, students who work while studying are said to be less anxious about their future prospects and show higher levels of career maturity than those students who do not work.

There is a growing body of evidence to suggest that, as the American model does, all learning in the workplace is valid and relevant, whether it be in the marketing department of a large organisation or serving behind the bar in the local pub. Many of the skills students learn while undertaking relatively menial work are transferable into more demanding workplaces.

Two-fifths (39%) of the respondents to a recent CRQ survey reported that they recognised that there are some benefits to be gained from working part-time during term-time (CRQ, 1997). Some students were unable to articulate what exactly was beneficial about working part-time: simply stating it was good work experience and would look impressive on their *curriculum vitae*. However, others differentiated between the different kinds of skills they had developed through their part-time job.

The evidence appears to suggest that part-time and vacation employment is a potential source of work experience that has not yet been fully explored by students, staff or employers. However, this may be about to change in light of Dearing's recommendation that all undergraduates should have the opportunity to experience work whilst at university (NCIHE, 1997). Indeed, there does seem to be a shift in employer perceptions, even in areas that have traditionally been more reserved about what constitutes valuable extracurricular activity:

A lot of students are working their way through university these days. I suppose they are getting something from their work outside university and that is something that shouldn't be sniffed at by universities. But they are only going to get some of these skills by being out in the workplace amongst other people. Maybe voluntary work, something like that, [would be a useful addition]. Anything that gets them out with other people in a work situation has got to help.

(Head of Branch, civil service)

Indeed, there seems to be a growing momentum from academics, careers advisors and employers to maximise the potential of part-time employment. For example, the idea of learning whilst earning from a part-time job was a major theme at a 1997 CRAC/CIHE conference 'Bridging the Work-Readiness Gap'.

Recognising the learning from TTPT and vacation employment may be one solution to the problem of expanding 'work placement' provision, an expansion that is unlikely to be met through more traditional sandwich courses alone. For example, Judith Evans (1997) reported that Sainsbury's are able to offer 130 placements per annum, 40 of which are traditional one-year placements and 70 are summer vacation placements prior to the final year. Sainsbury's are unable to expand these types of placement opportunities. However, they recognise that they have 35,000 under 25s working for Sainsbury's who are mostly in education. They are therefore developing a scheme aimed at accreditation of key skills in the workplace.

The notion of adapting part-time and vacation work that students do into a meaningful, beneficial and constructive activity is a contentious one. Even where higher education staff consider it as having some benefits in terms of enhancing skills, there is still a tendency to view it as something that is not really a meaningful part of undergraduate work as it does not relate to the subject matter of the course. This view makes it difficult to accredit it towards a higher education qualification.

However, there is a growing number of institutions that are recognising the potential learning associated with term-time, part-time, paid work, and are exploring the accreditation of such work. For example, Ripon and York St. John believe there may be some potential in accrediting TTPT work because some of their Film, Television, Literature and Theatre Studies students undertake jobs that are relevant to their course of study and possibly conducive to their future careers.

There is a difference between 'working' and 'work experience' as was discussed in Chapter 2. Work experience is part of a structured learning experience, it is more than just working in a setting outside the higher education institution. The key skills developed and the reflection undertaken on the learning process are crucial. Work experience is merely the means to these ends. Students need support in order to plan, reflect and articulate the learning that can be developed through TTPT and vacation work.

Reflection

Reflecting on the learning from work experience is crucial and this tends to be underdeveloped in most TTPT and vacation work.

I worked part-time in a fast-food restaurant. There is quite a lot of pressure. You must do what you have to do in a certain amount of time, otherwise you are going to let the whole thing down. I didn't find it too bad. I'm quite a methodical person, so if someone says, this is what you do and it's black and white and I can get on and do it, its only when I get woolly briefs that I get in trouble. I just sort of cracked on and did it. I learnt to keep a cool head and just to generally communicate well with people. So, I guess I did bring that to my current job. I think its quite difficult to recognise those skills because you just see it as a part-time job, you don't feel that you have got something out of it personally.

(Graduate Trainer, multi-national food manufacturers)

Those employers, academics and students who consider that TTPT and vacation work is, or can be, meaningful do so by concentrating on the learning undertaken rather than the type or level of work. The level of work-role responsibility may not necessarily determine at what level student learning may be taking place. Such learning will often encompass a range of personal and interactive skills such as working collaboratively, time- and self-management, learning about organisations and different employment environments.

> Something that has become apparent as I have been going round the universities, is that students are doing more and more part-time work in order to fund their time at university. A very common example would be working in a pub. We would be looking for people who can actually indicate that they have learned something from that. It is not just a chance to say: 'Well, it is to help pay off my overdraft'. In a pub you are dealing with people, cash, potentially difficult customers, you may be responsible for some other members of staff, you are working in a team as part of the bar staff. There is a lot of learning in there. It is what people are gleaning out of it, learning from it and are able to communicate to a selection panel.   (Graduate Recruitment Officer, large police force)

It is, thus, important to encourage and enable reflection on TTPT and vacation work. However, to do that, it has to be taken seriously. Circuitously, TTPT and vacation work will only be taken seriously, by academics, employers and students if students are able to reflect on and articulate the learning that derives from the experience.

The Community Enterprise module at Napier University takes the learning from TTPT voluntary work seriously. It provides the opportunity to accredit such work, discussed below, and provides a structure to encourage ongoing reflection. The primary purpose of this module is to develop transferable skills through giving students a basic level of experience of volunteering. It is supported by academic study of group theory and group dynamics, to encourage reflection on the students' role in the community organisation and their understanding of how the organisation works.

Similar reflection is embedded in the Tyneside and Northumberland 'Students into Schools' Project, where:

> Students are expected to become reflective practitioners, evaluating what they consider to be the most important aspects of the contribution they have made and identifying areas in which they feel this could be improved.   (Wood, 1997)

Although the academic staff, in such models, have taken a major role in encouraging and enabling reflection, it is also extremely helpful if support also comes from the employer as well. This, of course is even more crucial where the TTPT work is external to the programme of study. It has been suggested that in each employers' organisation there needs to be someone to help the reflective process and that TEC money could be used for this (Marshall, K. 1997).

Quality

Apart from those rare examples of voluntary TTPT work that have been developed into modules, it is very difficult to monitor the quality of this kind of work experience in terms of initial briefing, ongoing monitoring and debriefing. There are two features of such work that mitigate against any quality monitoring of the learning experience. First, the primary function of most TTPT and vacation paid work is to earn money. Second, most such work is obtained by the student approaching an employer directly without any university intermediary. Thus, the student will be unlikely to consider the learning opportunities at the outset and very unlikely to be in a position to negotiate a learning contract! A further problem, related specifically to vacation work, is that students are undertaking it whilst they have no contact with their university.

It may be, that with help, the student is able to subsequently reflect on the learning, even if only in retrospect, once the experience has passed. As was noted in Chapter 2, retrospective reflection, whilst better than nothing, is far less productive and far less indicative of a quality experience than ongoing reflection.

Of all the forms of work experience TTPT and vacation work is one where students have to take most responsibility, throughout the process, for monitoring the effectiveness of the learning through work. This requires an appreciation that learning is taking place and that it is worth reflecting upon and also a considerable self-discipline to document the reflection through an ongoing device such as a learning diary. However, despite the absence of guiding structure, there is also the very positive element that students will be developing as independent learners.

There is a need for structure and guidance to enable ongoing evaluation of the learning associated with TTPT and vacation work experience. Such a structure should be facilitated either through the employer, as in the ASDA 'Flying Start' scheme or through the higher education institution as, for example, in the developments at Napier University.

Assessment and accreditation of term-time, part-time work

There are a number of examples where institutions have started schemes to accredit the learning from TTPT work. This is typically an optional module where students gain credit from work they are already undertaking or subsequently undertake. This approach has been developed for both voluntary work and paid work. In both cases, the focus is on assessing the learning developed through undertaking the part-time work, rather than the particular tasks and processes undertaken. Initiatives recognising and accrediting the learning from voluntary work have, in some cases, been established more quickly than for paid TTPT work, probably because voluntary work is seen as a more legitimate extracurricular activity.

The Tyneside and Northumberland 'Students into Schools' Project has offered academic credit to a large number of student tutors since 1995. At the two universities involved, credit is equivalent to about one tenth of a degree year, and the student typically completes the tutoring module within one semester.

There are three components of the accreditation :

- formative logbook (including Personal Action Plan);
- summative formal written report;
- summative oral presentation.

All procedures and criteria for assessment are made clear in the form of a booklet, which participating students receive during their training sessions and at a briefing session part-way through the tutoring.

Napier University undertake similar accreditation of voluntary classroom assistants and also offer an accredited and assessed module, for about thirty students a year, in TTPT voluntary work in a not-for-profit agency (Highton, 1997).

Accreditation of TTPT voluntary work has also been developed external to the programme of study. For example, the National Union of Students has worked jointly with the National Centre for Work-Based Learning Partnerships to develop a Diploma in Professional Development (voluntary organisations) to be awarded by Middlesex University.

The Royal Society for Arts (RSA) have devised a scheme to offer NVQ accreditation for voluntary work. The RSA scheme places emphasis on key skills acquisition, rather than on the voluntary setting in which they are developed. The scheme aims to enable volunteers to gain a recognised qualification by on-the-job assessment of skills and competencies developed through a wide range of voluntary work. Work to be accredited within the scheme includes voluntary, community, leisure, home and family-based activities, which are not the candidate's paid work. This can include voluntary work undertaken during term time or vacations.

There are concerns that accrediting voluntary work will lead to a diminution of its intrinsic value. Such concerns relate to the work being its own reward and being disengaged from the academic programme.

There are some perceived disadvantages for students who tutor for credit rather than purely as volunteers. These include the diminished value of tutoring as a completely extra-curricular activity, the perceptions of extra 'pressure' on the quality of their tutoring, considerations of equable assessment and what happens if the placement does not run smoothly. However, the experience to date has indicated that, on balance, the additional time which is available to a student choosing a tutoring module – there is one less module from elsewhere – and the focus on self-assessment and personal development, outweigh the negative features.

(Wood, 1997)

Invariably, these attempts to accredit voluntary work have addressed themselves not to the nature of the work that is undertaken but what is learned from it, a feature that has been extended in the pioneering work on accrediting TTPT *paid* work at Napier University:

...I was trying to stand back and say, 'either the student is learning relevant things or they are not'. And, if they are, it's up to us to find a way of recognising that learning, assessing it and giving it credit, and holding on to that line without bothering too much with: is it voluntary? is it full-time?, is it part-time?, and all those other issues. So, drive through to focus on the learning. Is it relevant learning, relevant as far as the institution and the particular course is concerned? And if it is relevant how do we assess it? And if we can assess it, then how much credit do we give it? (Marshall, I., 1997)

The scheme at Napier involves an optional, 15-credit, level-one module, which accredits learning through part-time, paid employment. The onus is on the student to find the job. The project operates in conjunction with the university job bureau, which helps to advertise the scheme by suggesting to those students who register that they could get academic credit for the job they undertake. Students undertaking this module have to construct a learning contract with a number of learning outcomes. They have to negotiate an appropriate issue to address or problem to investigate.

A similar level-two, elective module is being developed at the University of Central Lancashire. Students are required to undertake 100 hours work experience and this can be part-time during term time or during their vacation. Students get credit for reflecting on the work and relating it to their curriculum. Students are therefore accredited for what they learn through the work, not for doing the work itself. It is up to the student to identify and apply for suitable work. However, it is acceptable for students to use the job they already have so long as they are able to prepare all the assessment material and show that they have reflected on both how they got the job and what they have learned from it. The nature or level of the work is irrelevant.

Students currently keep a series of 10 learning diaries, all of which are handed in for formative assessment, and four of which are used for formal assessment. Students also have to prepare a mock application pack and produce a lengthy final report, which is designed to be reflective and analytical. They are expected to reflect on their learning outcomes (agreed in a session prior to commencing the work). Students are encouraged to self-assess their skills in order to come up with their learning objectives. They are helped to reflect on what they already know and what they need in order to fulfil their career goals in the future.

Two problems have been highlighted. First, an ordinary taught module represents 140 hours; questions arise as to how much of the 140 hours is represented by 100 hours of work placement? What percentage of the working time is actually learning time? Second, a successful sandwich placement is one that is linked to the course curriculum and is not just a year out. The same can be said to be true of a shorter placement. As yet this module is not integral to programmes of study, it is a bolt-on module.

There is potential to expand the scheme at Napier and Central Lancashire. However, expanding such schemes starts to question taken-for-granteds about the location of learning.

Why restrict it to one 15-credit module? Why not say that if the student wishes they could take four 15-credit modules... In which case, in their one or two days with Napier, they might be taking a total of 60 credits through taught modules and have 60 credits they are picking up from the work, which they are having to do anyway to support themselves.... It's up to staff in Napier to be responding to that and to begin to have clarified in our own minds what constitutes appropriate chunks of relevant learning and appropriate evidence. That is by no means an overly challenging task because, at the moment, there are students who are spending half an academic year on placement, where, in effect, something like that is being done. It's just seen differently. A lot of this is paradigm shift – a different way of looking at it... I am trying to show that it can run efficiently and at relatively low cost, in order to make it attractive to other people within the institution, because clearly other people in the institution have to pick it up and run with it if it is going to become really big. The pilot is demonstrating that it can result in appropriate learning, effectively assessed, and can be managed at modest cost.

(Marshall, I., 1997)

However, even if students are willing to actively seek employment and tutors are willing to work out accreditation schemes, employers must also be committed to making the time spent in the work place meaningful for the student. Some employers are already starting to take this role seriously. For example, the ASDA 'Flying Start' programme involves students from their first year getting involved in a flexible working scheme for part-time work. Students are able to work in various aspects of the store under the tutelage of a store mentor or 'co-pilot'. The more hours they do the more points they accrue, points that can be cashed in for management training, for example.

Institutions are in a stronger position to understand and maximise the learning that occurs during term-time employment, that is not part of a programme of study, than students' learning through more traditional forms of vacation work.

Most accreditation, to date, of TTPT work is based on academic assessment of written or oral presentations about the nature of the work, rather than any direct assessment of the skills and abilities developed during the work, let alone any evaluation of task performance. An alternative approach to these elaborate procedures for accrediting part-time work is to suggest that if part-time or vacation work is to be incorporated into the academic environment it should be done through the national record of achievement or some form of profiling, which would simply serve as a record that the work experience had taken place and avoid the need to assess and accredit it (Marshall. K, 1997).

In essence, the issue of whether or not TTPT and vacation work is meaningful, credible and thus creditworthy rests on its legitimacy. Traditionally, such work was not included in the gamut of acceptable extra-curricular activities. With the exception of some forms of voluntary work, regarded as laudable for its altruism, term-time working in Britain is seen as an unwelcome incursion into the real activity of academia. It used to be considered that a full-time student should be a student full-time, not necessarily actively studying all hours but at least engaging in the academic milieu and interacting with other students on a full-time basis. Part-time working took students out of that milieu. The current, more flexible, structure of higher education, with a much less clearly defined difference between full- and part-time students, added to the enormous pressure on student finances, has cast doubt on traditional notions of extracurricular activity. Part-time work is gradually being accepted, if reluctantly, as a major element of extracurricular activity. However, there is a big difference between TTPT work achieving currency as extra-curricular activity and it becoming a legitimate and ultimately accredited form of work experience.

Barriers facing TTPT and vacation work

The main issue facing term-time part-time and vacation work is its legitimacy as an acceptable learning opportunity. The resource constraints that inhibit the developments of other forms of work experience are far less significant as there are already thousands of students undertaking part-time and vacation work. The barrier is whether or not the activity can or should be assimilated into the work-experience framework.

Is it a meaningful experience?

The view that TTPT and vacation work, especially paid work, is merely an inconvenience and does not constitute meaningful work experience is a significant barrier to the development of this kind of work experience. The low status of term-time, part-time work amongst academics and some employers is also reflected by the attitudes of some students to the unimportance of menial part-time work:

> Yes I worked in the University canteen. I was one of those people who went round with the trolley. It doesn't matter if you don't do it very well because you always know in the back of your mind it is not what you are going to do. When I was working [in a High Street Store], and I messed something up, it didn't matter, I was going at the end of the month.
>
> (Recent graduate, medium-sized brewing company)

One major concern for university staff and students is the lack of relevance to the subject of study. This distancing from the subject is problematic on three fronts.

First, the lack of subject-relevance not only disinclines some academics from taking an interest, there is often no structure within which to recognise the development of generic employability skills. In short, there is no clear locus for, or ownership of, the skills development process.

Second, lack of subject-relevance makes it more difficult for staff in higher education to assess, which is vital if it is to be formally accredited as part of the programme of study (Lee, 1997; Marshall, K., 1997). This is a symptom of a wider problem, in higher education, of assessment of skills other than 'higher-level' academic skills.

Third, until higher education outcomes are formulated in some form of profile or detailed record of achievement, then means of recording skills development, that are not embedded in assessed subject work, will be *ad hoc* or non-existent.

Rather more fundamentally, the National Centre for Work-Based Learning Partnerships, which can accredit some instances of paid work, takes the view that, on the whole, full-time students' experience in 'unskilled', part-time, paid work is often not of a sufficiently high level of learning to be accredited in their system. The National Centre's accreditation scheme is based on all higher education levels. It is difficult to equate student part-time working to these levels principally because students do not undertake specific projects, while working part-time, that can be assessed in accordance with the Centre's assessment criteria (Naish, 1997). Interestingly, voluntary part-time work often offers more focused activity that is project-based.

These views of the validity of TTPT work are echoed by some employers, who regard 'appropriate' work experience as only that experience pertinent to the specific realm of employment:

> *When you are looking for graduates, is prior work experience an element that you consider important?*
> Yes, but a relevant work placement, I would say. We get a lot come who have had work placement but they've worked in fast-food restaurants or supermarkets.
>
> (Partner, small private design consultancy)

> If all graduates doing a course could be found some kind of [relevant] work experience to do during the summer vacation rather than having to do mundane things, it would obviously be better because you would be learning something. Coming here, putting things together, was better for me than working in a shop or picking potatoes.
>
> (Electrical engineer, small medical lasers manufacturer)

Resources

Although resources are not the main barrier they are still important. The key resource issue is the lack of funding to capture the learning from TTPT and vacation work. For example, there are student employment agencies that help to find students part-time work and, to some extent, also ensure conditions of employment. However, most say that, although they are aware that learning takes place, they do not have the funds to be able to play a role in preparation, or identification and articulation of the learning. Although some organisations have produced 'skills trackers' they do not see them as simply self-completion exercises but acknowledge the need for students to receive guidance and support when articulating learning (STEP, nd; AIESEC, 1998).

Through the establishment of University Job Shops, higher education institutions are showing an awareness of increasing student hardship and the need for students to work during term-time. Some job shops have been established by the university and some have been set up by student unions. There are now around 56 similar organisations across the sector (with another 20 in the process of being set up). Examples include: TEMPUS, University of Sheffield; NUCLEUS, University of Nottingham; The Jobshop, University of Huddersfield; The Job Bureau, University of Central England; Student Job Shop, University of Newcastle; Student Job Shop; University College, Winchester; Clearing House, The University of Edinburgh; USE Bureau, Wolverhampton University.

These bureaux are not employment agencies, rather they simply display vacancies. Occasionally they match students to jobs, particularly if the position requires specialist skills. However, the majority of jobs are unskilled positions, which are displayed and anyone registered with the bureau may apply.

Student employment bureaux are set up partly in response to increasing student hardship and partly as a means to provide students with work experience. However, although some of the positions, particularly full-time, summer placements, are highly skilled, of an appropriate higher education level and often course relevant, these bureaux are not equipped to offer students any form of academic accreditation for the experience. Many would like to but have not got the resources.

The only monitoring that usually takes place relates to pay and conditions. Most bureaux have a minimum wage of around £3 per hour and will refuse to display jobs offering less than that. Many also place a ceiling of 15 hours per week on the jobs they display. This is part of the job shops' commitment to protect academic standards and it is taken as axiomatic that this is the primary concern.

There is enormous variety in the administrative structures of student employment services, some being based in students' unions, others in careers services, others in university administration departments, often with advisory groups including representatives of the local key players. The development of these services has 'muddied the waters' in terms of relations with employers because there is yet another network of contacts, separate from the placement officers in some academic departments. AGCAS has recognised the need for internal collaboration and now has a Student Employment Services Working Party to monitor developments and to share good practice.

For voluntary work, an increase in student hardship may mean that students have less time to be able to undertake voluntary work. Increased pressure to earn money during term-time may restrict students in following a particular interest or commitment through part-time voluntary work.

Summary

It needs to be acknowledged that work and home commitments play an increasing role for both full-time and part-time undergraduates and these experiences need to be recognised as playing a part in the student's whole learning process. Recognising the learning opportunity from term-time, part-time and vacation work presents the most radical potential for change in the understanding and use of work experience for and by undergraduates.

- Term-time, part-time (TTPT) and vacation work is either paid or voluntary. Increasing student hardship is the main reason for an increasing number of students undertaking paid work. Reasons for undertaking voluntary work include: to pursue a particular interest; to make a contribution to society; to develop particular skills; and, to get some experience.

- *Benefits to employers and voluntary organisations* of students undertaking TTPT and vacation work include having a pool of flexible labour they can call on as required, which is intelligent, quick to learn and good 'value for money'. Furthermore, students working part-time also provide a potential recruitment opportunity.

- Some *students* recognise that, in addition to the money, there are associated benefits to earning while learning. TTPT and vacation work may also be an opportunity for students to gain work experience and develop employability skills, which they can use to good effect in recruitment interviews.

- There are also specific benefits associated with the work being undertaken on a voluntary basis, which include: the opportunity to undertake rewarding work experience; recognition from employers of the contribution made by people undertaking work for the good of others; an opportunity to broaden experience; and, in some cases, the development of a range of delicate or specific, client-sensitive interactive skills.

- *Benefits to staff in higher education* include the fact that students have already found the work. This saves the institution a lot of money in terms of the cost of identifying suitable placements for the students. Students undertaking TTPT or vacation work on a voluntary basis may also provide an opportunity for staff to develop links between the institution and the community.

- Whether TTPT or vacation work, particularly when it's paid work, offers a 'meaningful' experience for students is a contentious issue. TTPT is rarely seen as part of an *intended* learning experience. Various studies highlight the negative impact on students' academic work of working part-time, a view often reinforced by academics.

- However, there is a growing body of evidence to suggest that all learning in the workplace is valid and relevant. Many of the skills students learn while undertaking relatively menial work are transferable into more demanding workplaces. The level of work role responsibility may not necessarily determine at what level student learning may be taking place. Such learning will often encompass a range of personal and interactive skills.

- Term-time, part-time and vacation employment may be one solution to the problem of expanding 'work placement' provision, an expansion that is unlikely to be met through more traditional sandwich courses alone. However, there is a difference between 'working' and 'work experience'. Work experience is part of a structured learning experience, it is more than just working in a setting outside the higher education institution. The keys are the skills that have been developed, the reflection undertaken and the articulation of the learning experience. Work experience itself is merely the means to these ends.

- Of all the forms of work experience, TTPT and vacation work is one where students have to take most responsibility, throughout the process, for monitoring the effectiveness of the learning through work.

- There is a need for structure and guidance to enable ongoing evaluation of the learning associated with TTPT and vacation work experience. Such a structure should be facilitated either through the employer or through the higher education institution.

- There are a number of examples where institutions have started schemes to accredit the learning from TTPT work. This is typically an optional module where students gain credit from work they are already undertaking or subsequently undertake. This approach has been developed for both voluntary work and paid work. In both cases, the focus is on assessing the learning developed through undertaking the part-time work, rather than the particular tasks and processes undertaken.

- There is a small but increasing demand from students to have their TTPT work accredited. Accreditation at present appears to be initiated at the programme level by academics, although there are some examples of employers taking the initiative, such as ASDA's Flying Start scheme.

- Institutions are in a stronger position to understand and maximise the learning that occurs during term-time employment, that is not part of the course of study, than learning through more traditional forms of vacation work.

- Even if students are willing to actively seek employment and tutors are willing to work out accreditation schemes, employers must also be committed to making the time spent in the work place meaningful for the student.

- Most accreditation, to date, of TTPT work is based on academic assessment of written or oral presentations. An alternative approach is to suggest that if part-time or vacation work is to be incorporated into the academic environment it should be done through the national record of achievement or some form of profiling.

- The main barrier inhibiting the realisation of the learning potential of term-time part-time and vacation work is its perceived legitimacy as an acceptable learning opportunity.

- Although resources are not the main barrier they are still important. There is a need for funding to aid students in *capturing* the learning from TTPT and vacation work.

6 Summary and recommendations

There are considerable benefits of work experience for employers, students and academic staff but there are also costs associated with involvement in work experience. These costs constitute barriers to the expansion of work experience. This chapter summarises:

- the overall benefits of work experience to employers, students and academic staff;
- the barriers to expansion, which are linked to the 'costs' of providing work experience;
- some of the possible resolutions;

This is followed by recommendations for future action.

Benefits and costs of work experience

Employers

For employers, there is the benefit of extra workers at low cost. Students may be employed undertaking 'everyday' work or it may be the opportunity to set up a new project or get something completed that has been on the 'back-burner'.

> I think a lot more companies should be involved in industrial placement skills even though it is only for six months it is cheap labour. You can get an undergraduate who is doing a six-months placement to do just the same job as a graduate at half the salary.
>
> (Car Fleet Manager, multinational reprographic equipment manufacturer)

Work experience provides the possibility that students might contribute an injection of new ideas into the organisation.

It also has potential recruitment benefits in providing the opportunity for employers to give a potential recruit a trial without obligation:

> We have a summer placement programme for students. If they do a placement with us obviously that is the optimum solution. It provides the student with an opportunity to see how they like us and how we like them. And it provides us with an opportunity to see how the student operates within the environment. If it is with another company it is still worthwhile as well, because by questioning the graduates on how they saw their work experience and how they viewed the hands-on experience, that is very useful information in the recruitment process.
>
> (Dealer Analyst, multi-national petro-chemical company)

Some employers approach work experience in a more general sense, by using students' reflection on any work experience as a recruitment criterion. They see the benefit in having a pool of potential recruits with some general awareness of workplace culture:

> With some of the three-year courses I think it is essential that people are encouraged to look at businesses and look at how they work. This year we have a summer placement scheme. We have somebody here for eight weeks in her summer holiday who is actually getting paid and is looking at a possible career in retail management and is utilising her holidays to have an insight into that. But we interviewed her the same as we would a graduate, exactly the same, to make sure that she still had the skills required to operate in the system. With things like that, it is really important that industry and education actually link, to build more of these opportunities, because it is a big difference from a sheltered environment of study: you are on your own and when you are out there it is every person for themselves.
>
> (Assistant Personnel Manager, large international retailers)

Work experience is also a means by which employers can develop links with higher education institutions for a range of things, including research and development through to targeting 'high-flyer' recruits.

> My colleagues tell me the trick is to get into the higher education, get links into the departments, into the staff who are in there, and then you start to identify the better students.
>
> (Personnel Director, multi-national engineering company)

Work-experience students can also add value indirectly. Employers with a well-developed work-experience culture gain the benefit of enhancement of current staff through mentorship. Perhaps the best examples are to be found in professional areas such as nursing, clinical placements, teaching and social work, where providers have a clear commitment to continuing professional development through supervision of staged placements. Although providers are not without their own particular resourcing problems, they do have a well-established culture of learning in the workplace (albeit regulated by statute) that acts in the interest of the profession. In some areas, such as nursing, placement students are an invaluable additional resource.

Many employers, of course, do not have the experience, tradition or culture of input from professional bodies, yet still manage to invest in, and benefit from, a learning culture within the organisation, both in terms of providing opportunities for students and using such opportunities to develop their staff. However, for SMEs the lack of resources to invest in training and development is a real barrier to their progression as learning organisations:

> We have got very small resources for training development and we would really like to build that in the future and kick off more of a learning culture.
>
> (Line Manager, medium-sized insurance company)

In summary, *benefits for employers* include:

- extra workers at low cost;
- the setting up of a new project;
- the completion of specific tasks;
- the opportunity to give a potential recruit a trial without obligation;
- using students' reflection on work experience as a recruitment criterion;
- having a pool of potential recruits with some general awareness of workplace culture;
- an injection of new ideas;
- developing links with higher education institutions;
- staff development opportunities that arise from employees mentoring students.

Students

For *students*, the benefits of work experience include the opportunity to work in a setting where theory, learned on a programme of study, is put into practice.

> I applied for a summer job here and worked for 11 weeks within the firm, two weeks of training and then 6–7 weeks on a client site, working with real people [from the firm] and real clients. And the clients didn't know that I was a student so I had to fulfil the role of a consultant, which was really good experience for me. I classed it as the longest second interview ever, over 8–9 weeks, where the firm got a chance to see how I worked under pressure and in a real client environment. I had a good taste of what life with [the firm] would be like if I did decide to join.
>
> (New graduate, large management consultants)

Such opportunities benefit students by giving them the chance to develop an awareness of work-place culture and an appreciation of the fluidity of a rapidly changing world of work.

Work experience also helps to enhance the learning through their studies at university as it can provide students with the opportunity to develop or enhance a range of *personal attributes* such as time-management, self confidence and adaptability. In addition, work experience helps develop *interactive attributes*, notably teamworking, interpersonal skills and communication including the enhancement of ability to use information technology and, in some cases, language development. The development of personal and interactive skills enhances the graduates' work readiness. Work experience provides the opportunity to develop these attributes in a workplace context to an extent that goes beyond what is normally available through the academic element of programmes of study.

For some students, work experience provides short-term financial benefit as they are earning whilst studying, thus helping to reduce student hardship. In the longer run, students have the prospect of enhanced employment prospects and the potential of commanding higher wages when starting employment after graduation as their work experience is often regarded positively by recruiters.

Work experience provides students with assistance in developing career strategies, such as help with career choice.

It also helps students to become more aware of opportunities and to build up a network of contacts:

> Basically I don't think I would have got this job without having done the work experience. It gives you the chance to make contacts within a company, to discover all sorts of new aspects that you didn't know about before and to actually find out what working in a pharmaceutical company is like. (Assistant Research Scientist, large pharmaceutical manufacturers)

In some cases, work experience, especially abroad, has the benefit of living and working in another culture, learning other languages and contributing to the global community.

In summary, the *benefits for students* include:

- working in a setting in which to put theory into practice;
- developing an awareness of work-place culture;
- an appreciation of the fluidity of a rapidly changing world of work;
- an opportunity to develop a range of *personal attributes*;
- the development of key *interactive attributes*;
- short-term financial benefits – some students are earning whilst studying, thus helping to reduce student hardship;
- enhanced employment prospects and the potential of commanding higher wages when starting employment after graduation;
- assistance in developing career strategies, such as help with career choice;
- becoming aware of opportunities and building up a network of contacts;
- living and working in another culture, learning other languages and contributing to the global community.

Staff in higher education

For *staff in higher education institutions*, benefits of work experience include the opportunity for students to see their subject area in a practical setting. This, in turn, can provide increased student commitment to, and understanding of, their academic studies upon their return to their course. They are also likely to obtain satisfaction from seeing students develop and mature as a result of the development of a range of skills and abilities in the workplace setting:

> What they can get on the placement that they can't get here is working with people who do it for a living. That means they have to get it right first time, they have a different approach to ideas, it is much more cut-throat. If it is not going to earn them money then they can't really afford to do it. It is the market place aspect. On top of that there are things like better access to equipment, contacts for future work and those sorts of spin-offs. (Kemp, 1997)

Academics are able to benefit from the establishment of links with a wider range of employers, which may lead to a fresh approach to various aspects of the programme of study and to help ensure that commercial or industry-related teaching is up-to-date. It may lead to research initiatives or consultancy opportunities. Links may also encourage employers to participate on course validation panels in the development of subject areas, present guest lectures or participate in seminars, all of which increase course relevance.

Academics may benefit from closer links with employers through the creation and tailoring of innovative or more applicable work experiences. These links can help to identify ways in which students could be more effectively prepared for work in the future.

> Companies need to feed back to the universities. Maybe the company could feed back to the university about the graduates the year after they have been working to give a general report on the graduate covering extra skills the university could have provided – to have some sort of ongoing communication between the universities and the employer after employment. (Car Fleet Manager, multinational reprographic equipment manufacturer)

Work experience links may also be a basis for helping academics develop their expertise in assessment methods by working with employers who have experience in assessing 'employability' skills.

In summary, *benefits for academics* in higher education institutions include:

- the opportunity for students to see their subject area in practice;
- the satisfaction of seeing students develop and mature;
- the enhancement of students' skills;
- the establishment of links with a wider range of employers, with the potential for bringing a fresh approach to higher education institutions;
- using employer contacts to ensure that their commercial or industry-related teaching is up-to-date;
- using links to encourage employers to participate on course validation panels in the development of subject areas, present guest lectures or participate in seminars;
- the creation and tailoring of innovative or more applicable work experiences through collaboration with past employers of placement students;
- developing their expertise in assessment methods by working with employers who have experience in assessing 'employability' skills.

Barriers

Although work experience has significant benefits, the associated costs lead to a number of barriers to expansion. These barriers fall into three broad areas:

- resources;
- organisation;
- creating opportunities.

In summarising these barriers, some possible resolutions are identified.

Resources

A lack of resources appears to be the biggest barrier to the expansion of work experience for all stakeholders. In an ideal world, there would be sufficient funds to enable employers to provide students with work-experience opportunities, supported by well-funded higher education institutions with full backing from the government. Clearly this will not happen. As Brennan and Little (1996) stated, 'a crucial question remains as to whether higher education institutions and employers can afford such an investment'. In the light of proposed changes in funding, this question is more critical than ever.

The lack of resources impacts in a variety of ways. First, the resource implications to employers for providing undergraduates with work experience. Second, the cost implications for the student. Third, the resource implications for academic staff and higher education institutions.

Stakeholders are having to take pragmatic steps to deal with the 'work readiness' problem of new graduates. Many employers and higher education institutions have demonstrated innovative ways of approaching the problems of helping students to gain from a variety of work-experience opportunities. Although resourcing is a huge barrier, if students, and ultimately graduate employees, are to be seen as a human resource worthy of investment for the future, there are ways of maximising the potential. What is crucial is that any expansion does not compromise the quality of the learning experience.

Employers

Although employers benefit from the provision of work experience, they also face costs. These costs include the amount of time that is necessary to supervise a student, to set-up and to monitor projects or work tasks that students undertake.

> We are a very streamlined organisation and you find that you don't have as much time to be involved with work placements as you would like. But we are very keen and do take an active interest in these sort of areas and it is really only the time constraints that prevents us getting more involved. (Training and Personnel Manager, medium-sized private broadcasting company)

There are also costs in terms of the time and effort it takes to make links with higher education institutions and subsequently the potential students:

> We had a spate of students wanting to come on work placements, and we arranged for three and none of them wanted to do it in the end, which was annoying.
>
> (Owner, small design consultancy)

In addition there are, in some circumstances, high costs in establishing an appropriate work-station for work-experience students.

> We used to take on a number of sandwich students, we take less on now. The big problem now is that in the old days you gave the technical designer either a relatively cheap computer or a drawing board and a bit of software and they could get on and do some work and design. The capital cost has increased and increased over the years, as computer power increases, and currently it costs us about £40k a seat to have a designer. Now we can't afford to invest £40k worth of capital equipment. Half of that is hardware and you can write that off over two years. (Managing Director, medium-sized shop-fitting manufacturer)

Finally, for some employers, the requirement, on some forms of work experience, to pay the students a wage or a consultancy fee is seen as an additional cost, even when the amounts in question are relatively small.

For many employers, the initial reaction to work experience tends to be that the process has resource implications, and that, in effect the benefits are a gamble. Thus resources are not just an accounting barrier they are also a psychological barrier to the expansion of work-experience opportunities. The actual financial costs are usually not high and students may actually save employers money. There are many documented cases of this happening (Chapters 3 and 4). Offering work-experience opportunities to undergraduates may also be a cheap recruitment tool, as many firms have found out.

However, it is not so much the financial cost as the time element that is a major inhibitor. The time that has to be invested, particularly up-front, is sometimes seen as a major barrier to expansion of work-experience opportunities, particularly for relatively short placements or projects. This is especially the case for SMEs who do not have the infrastructure to support a work-experience student, and would want them to be effective from day one, much as when they recruit new staff.

How would you feel about that, having someone on, say a work placement for a year, or a half year?

My initial reaction would be to say that it would be a bit of an overhead for me today, in the sense that I would have to invest. There is no point in this person coming unless they gain from it. To do that they are going to have some on-the-job training and so on. From my view, they need to get the opportunity to have a go at contributing in some way, to help make it more realistic and worthwhile, and therefore, it will be a significant investment for my department, and potentially, therefore, the company. Looking at it very selfishly, I would get very little back from my investment. However, I recognise I ought to look at it more globally and say it would be good for the company in the long run, and certainly good for the country. However I would want to put the company first, almost certainly.

(Team Manager, medium-sized software services contractor)

However, such reservations assume that the up-front costs are wasted. What is needed is for employers, especially added-value employers, to change the way that they look at work experience for students. A major barrier occurs when work experience is 'sold' as solely of benefit to students: relying on employer altruism. In reality, work-experience students are a benefit to employers. If students are seen as a resource, rather than as a nuisance, employers are making a positive investment for the future. There are real-life examples of companies who have seen an impact on their 'bottom line' as a result of work placement. The experience of the Shell STEP programme has shown that students can act as agents of change, help improve the efficiency and performance of small companies, with minimal cost (Cunningham, 1997).

Some graduate recruiters, notably large retailers, recognise not just the need to keep pace with rapid changes, but to anticipate future changes. They are part of a service industry that faces intense competition on a global scale. The use of new technology, such as self-scanning techniques and selling through the Internet, means that it is crucial for their workforces to have relevant skills to keep the competitive edge. Such employers are looking to develop their existing workforce by utilising an existing pool of part-time staff, many of whom are students working part-time during term time to survive (Evans, 1997; Horn, 1997) (Chapter 5).

Where benefits outweigh costs, employers are more inclined to offer work-experience opportunities. Where the perception is that costs outweigh benefits then employers are less inclined to get involved. However, perceived benefits and costs are not simple issues, and depend, amongst other things, on the structure, flexibility and ethos of the employer organisation, the extent of its links with higher education, its recruitment strategy, its commitment to lifelong learning and approach to staff development and training.

Students

Although the benefits for students are substantial, there are also costs including additional living costs and travel costs, the payment of fees on placement years and the opportunity cost, in some cases, of deferring earnings for another year.

Under the present funding system, student hardship is a factor that may deter students from entering higher education. Students who are not deterred now have to give very careful consideration to the kinds of courses they choose and may be against opting for four-year sandwich courses and facing an extra year's debt. A paid one-year placement may help to alleviate student debt but many potential sandwich students may not want to risk an extra year in the hope of getting a well-paid placement. The proposed introduction of fees and the requirement for placement students to pay up to £500 for the placement year (Clarke, 1997) may further reduce demand for sandwich courses. This seems a considerable sum for the level of support that many students get whilst on placement. Students may be better off taking a break from the programme and working for a year. Indeed, the Student Sponsorship Officer at the University of Warwick (based in the Careers Advisory Service) reports that during recent years there is a growing trend to take time out during their courses (Cox, 1997). A combination of financial imperatives and the wish to gain greater motivation for their academic studies are the most common motives.

In the light of the Government's proposal to introduce fees for tuition there is a general anxiety among all stakeholders about the impact this will have on the student population. The National Union of Students are concerned that:

> ...the proposals will deter many potential students from entering higher education, especially those from less well-off backgrounds.
>
> (West Midlands Area NUS, 1997)

However, for some students, the costs are not financial but a more intellectually and emotionally demanding academic experience as a result of mixing 'real world' working with academia. The problems of attempting to balance academic work with the pressures of a 'real' work situation are seen as too risky by some students who consider that the work experience adds little in comparison with the disruption it causes to a period of intensive academic study:

> Work experience is probably quite a good idea: well, certainly over the summer vacation. I don't think I would want to take a year out, because of the learning thing, coming to work you are learning different things, it is not academic, and I think you would lose the academic momentum. It's the same reason for not having a break between 'A levels' and university. Yes, summer vacation is all right but I don't think I would have wanted to do it for much longer than that. I think it would break it too much.
>
> (Electrical Engineer, small medical lasers manufacturer)

Some students are afraid that work experience would result in excessive work load or repetitive, tedious or otherwise 'inappropriate' work. However, increasingly, students who engage in paid work during term time have little choice but to tolerate the 'reality' of hardship.

The weighting of the different benefits and costs will depend on the motivation for the work experience, and indeed, whether the work undertaken during an undergraduate programme is even viewed as 'work experience'. Term-time, part-time work, for example, may not be seen as 'appropriate' work experience, it may be viewed as simply a means of earning money and so costs, such as tedium, that would not be endured as part of a course-embedded placement, may be tolerated as part of paid external work.

However, students should note that employers value all forms of work experience provided that students can articulate what they have learned in the process. Therefore, they should not be afraid of mentioning part-time work but should be clear about the learning outcomes before, during and after the work experience.

Higher education staff

There are many innovative ways in which stakeholders can use resources to invest in learning in the workplace (examples in Chapters 3–5). It can be argued that such innovation, or lack of it, reflects the level of commitment to change.

This lack of commitment is, in part, a result of the costs to academics of involvement in work experience. The time and effort required to establish and maintain links with employers is considerable, as is the subsequent time to monitor, assess and evaluate work-experience situations. For example, research in the area of 'Leisure', found that, 'although desirable in theory', some institutions did not offer 'placements' as part of the course. The reasons for not doing so included 'administration problems caused by modularisation', which make it difficult to arrange placements' and 'insufficient resources from the institution to ensure a quality experience for the student' (Jones, Hunter Jones, and Callander, 1996).

Furthermore, academic staff rarely get appropriate credit for this type of activity. Indeed, there is a general lack of recognition, within higher education institutions, of the effort required to liaise with employers.

The lack of recognition is reflected in a lack of reward, in terms of status or pay, for the responsibility for co-ordinating work experience. It is also evident in the lack of funding generally available to support work-experience initiatives.

However, lack of commitment to work experience is often indicative of a reluctance in higher education institutions to accept that learning can take place in a variety of settings – there is an implicit hierarchy of learning that ranks 'learning' in the lecture hall above all other methods. A commitment to a wider view of learning, rather than teaching, and conceptualising work experience as part of the learning process is necessary to overcome a major barrier. According to Brennan and Little (1996), 'learning acquired at work is as valid as learning acquired by any other means'. However, this is not the view of many academics who have to be convinced of the value of learning outside the academic context.

The role of the academic tutor has changed and continues to do so. In addition to their role in the facilitation of learning for an increasing number of students, academic staff face a burgeoning administrative burden. It is not surprising, then, that they resist being 'lumbered' with the complex task of managing work-experience opportunities, for which there may be little relief from teaching and little prospect of promotion.

In higher education, resource issues are a day-to-day reality that need careful and responsible management. Higher education institutions have found themselves in a market place competing nationally and globally against each other for students. To survive, they must ensure that the courses on offer satisfy 'customer' needs.

Meeting 'customer' needs will have a particular resonance for students on sandwich courses as they are required to pay fees towards placement years. There will, doubtless, be an increased emphasis on the student as a customer with the associated rights to a quality service. As a consequence, there is likely to be increased pressure on resources, resulting in a possible disinclination of staff, and maybe institutions as a whole, to become involved in lengthy, course-embedded work experience.

Higher education institutions accommodate work experience in a variety of ways (Appendix 1). Some of these, such as traditional sandwich placement years, are funded (at least in part). However, it seems that not all the money that is earned to support work experience is actually used to resource such opportunities:

> We are very committed to placements and we have always done an awful lot of it, but whether we invest in it is a totally different issue... I have no evidence whatsoever, that any, other than the most basic of that money, goes into supporting a placement or the structure that supports placements... We are working on a policy document now and one of the things we said right at the beginning is that we cannot implement this unless the resource is there. And people started saying 'Oh, the resources are there' – well the resources are there because they come through the student fee, at the moment of course, but they are not being put into that. What we are saying is that the money that comes in must be re-invested...   (Challis, 1997)

Brennan and Little (1996, p. 102) questioned whether institutions are prepared to redistribute resources and use them in different ways. The resourcing implications of providing work experience go beyond the administrative costs of setting up opportunities for students and liaising with host organisations and the costs of supervising or visiting students during a period of work experience. There are additional costs of enhancing work experience, improving quality assurance processes, developing staff and enhancing and focusing assessment procedures. It is crucial that this issue is faced and tackled if Dearing recommendations on work experience are to be implemented.

Academics in different areas or different institutions will have varying views on the importance of different costs and benefits, and will be more or less inclined to overcome the resource barriers. For some, the contacts and influences that are built up through work experience collaborations are essential for maintaining the relevance of courses and enabling staff to keep abreast of changes in the field (Knapper and Cropley, 1985). For others, work experience is something that detracts from the teaching of the 'subject matter' or from the time to undertake research, which attracts far more reward and kudos.

Organisation

A key question that has emerged from the research is, whose role should it be to develop links with employers, and to organise and manage work experience within higher education institutions? Should this be a function of academic staff within teams or departments, in addition to their teaching load? Is 'placing' students a straightforward administrative role? Is it a highly specialised liaison or marketing role that may warrant considerable investment in terms of resources by higher education institutions? Should the careers service play a key role in helping students to find work-experience opportunities, as the Dearing Committee suggests (NCIHE, 1997)?

This dilemma was recognised by Watts (1997), who raised the question, 'what is the scope within institutions for integrating placement work on exit with course-related placements and placements on part-time and vacation jobs?'

Management of work experience opportunities

It would appear that there are considerable variations of practice in higher education institutions in relation to the facilitation of work-experience opportunities. It appears that work experience tutors may be 'all shades of everything' (Challis, 1997), and 'what exists is scattered, diverse and of variable quality' (QSC, 1996).

> A [work experience] tutor's job tends to be the one that people are sidelined into. It is not a high prestige job, it is not a supported job...They don't necessarily see themselves involved in teaching and learning. (Challis, 1997)

According to Quality Support Centre's (1996) *Signposts for Staff Development (1)*, the link tutor can be defined as:

> A representative of the educational institution linking that institution with a workplace organisation which is actively involved in delivering significant elements of the educational programme provided for students. The link tutor fulfils a variety of roles in relation to students and workplace personnel, including overall responsibility for the management of the placement itself. (QSC, 1996, (1))

This work is done either by administrative staff or academic staff or, sometimes, by teams consisting of both administrators and academics. It is mostly an activity located within schools or departments. Although the role does not usually carry high status, the tasks and responsibilities require a variety of skills that are crucial to the effectiveness of the operation and may require a dedicated team of people to meet the demands of the job:

> ...what is happening in many places is that the work that used to be done by academics in relation to placements is being passed on to administrative staff. That is not unreasonable, because there are lots of tasks which good administrators can do much better than academics, many of whom give low priority to administration. But good administrators are not cheap. (Lee, 1997)

> The Business School is the only faculty to have a full-time placement office as such. I think all the other departments [in other faculties] have just got an academic with a partial remission on their timetable to handle placements. So, in a lot of cases, they have to be reactive. They have to react to things that come along to them rather than be pro-active and go out and look for things because it is incredibly time-consuming. (Thorn, 1997)

Indeed it has been suggested that 'the link tutor holds the reins of quality assurance process for learning in the workplace' (QSC, 1996). The actual job may involve an individual or team of people in a variety of tasks, many of which involve helping students to prepare for work experience. In addition, the role may involve public relations and marketing to persuade employers of the benefits:

> It is difficult to develop links with people because it takes so much time, and up until now we have not had to develop them to get the best graduates, probably because there are a lot of graduates around. If we found we were getting very short of graduates we would develop more links, but it is a matter of whether it is cost effective. A few years ago we actually brought in the course tutors here and showed them round and gave them lunch, to try and encourage them to get their best graduates to come and work here, but we don't do that now.
>
> (Operations Manager, computer-controlled systems manufacturer)

There is hot competition for 'work-experience opportunities' both within and between institutions. Academics and administrators in higher education institutions involved in work experience tend to be very precious about links with employers in case someone 'steals' a contact. Research at Nottingham Trent University on sharing placement contacts canvassed staff views about whether they would share contacts with other departments and institutions. The majority (92%) of staff said they would share contacts with other departments, although a smaller majority (73%) actually did. When staff were asked whether they would share with other faculties, 83% said they would but only 53% actually did. Less than a quarter (21%) said they would share with other universities, and only 13% actually did (Yarwood, 1997).

There appears to be an ongoing debate about the complementarity of the role of 'placement' managers and careers advisers. It has been suggested that careers services could co-ordinate work experience. In many ways they are well-placed to undertake the role as many of the employers with whom they have developed contacts for recruitment purposes are also likely to be able to offer work experience of some type. Careers services are also used to helping students interpret and articulate a wide range of experiences on their *curriculum vitae*, applications forms and interviews. However, they would require additional resources to adequately fulfil this wider remit.

It would not be appropriate for careers services to take responsibility for placements that are a compulsory part of academic programmes. Whilst work experience forms an important part of career education and planning, placement and careers advice are seen as two separate functions because one of the strengths of careers services is that their staff give impartial advice to students acting as 'honest brokers', an element emphasised by the Dearing Committee (NCIHE, 1997). Giving guidance about the value of all types of work experience, information sources, obtaining new opportunities and promoting them are all quite different from being involved in the selection and placement of specific students, or assessing their experience. Hence the view expressed by the majority of the members of the Executive Committee of the Association of Graduate Recruiters, for example, that the most appropriate place for placements that are part of the academic programme is at faculty level, although they recognised that SMEs, in particular, would benefit from a more centralised approach to higher education-employer links.

Lack of co-operation between careers and placement officers is sometimes evident when it comes to sharing work experience opportunities. This tension was sensed by one graduate employer:

> Careers services and industrial placement tutors are both ideally working for the benefit of students, but as an employer I detect the signs of non-co-operation.
>
> (Graduate Recruiter, AGR Conference, 1997)

Often, careers services try to keep academic departments informed of contacts but this is rarely reciprocated especially if industrial contacts are being nurtured with a view to developing research contracts as well as work experience opportunities. Some institutions are recognising these problems and are working on solutions. For example, at the University of Warwick the Student Sponsorship Officer is a member of the Careers Advisory Service staff and is responsible for building and maintaining an extensive work-experience database of opportunities for year-long and shorter placements, sponsorship of various types, work shadowing, vacation courses, programmes such as STEP and a wide variety of traditional and non-traditional options. Employers interested in offering work-experience opportunities can receive personalised advice and enquirers are referred to other appropriate university staff.

The use of technology in the work experience process helps to ensure that both students and employers are dealt with in a professional manner and that up-to-date information is available. However, it is vital that link tutors are aware of, and have access to, these opportunities and are able to advise and direct students to them. Staff need to have access to the information technology resources required to function in the most effective manner (Yarwood, 1997).

Communication

There is a problem of information flows, often exacerbated by unclear identification of roles within higher education institutions and employing organisations. One of the biggest barriers, according to graduate employers seeking to provide a work-experience opportunity for a student, is the absence in higher education institutions of a 'one-stop' communication point, where they can make contact with someone who can provide them with information. Higher education institutions rarely have very clear policies or systems that enable information flows. Often contacts are personal and disappear when personnel change. Such a lack of communication may lead not just to a duplication of effort, but may discourage employers if they have no clear point of contact. It would be a significant improvement in higher education-employer links if institutions put in place a 'one-stop' communication point. However, this does require clear points of contact within the institution and good communication flows.

The National Committee of Inquiry into Higher Education identified the issue of making information accessible to employers:

> We recommend to HEIs and their representative bodies that they examine, with representatives of industry, ways of giving firms, especially SMEs, easy and co-ordinated access to information about higher education services in their areas.   (NCIHE, 1997, Recommendation 38)

Employers, particularly SMEs and employers who have had little previous contact with higher education, may not know what they want. They may find the confusion, and the time and effort involved, too much and may turn to an alternative institution or even forget the whole idea.

Similarly, a lack of clear information available for students can result in students missing out on worthwhile work experience opportunities:

> When I was at university I didn't know you could get a job [here] for the summer. Why didn't I know about that? I was active in looking around at the careers service, but I didn't know you could get a job with this firm for the summer – why?

> (Graduate Trainee, large international corporate accountants)

As a result, students may be unaware of the range of work experience available and how they can get involved. Responsibilities for different forms of work experience rest with a variety of departments within different institutions. Some student associations have responsibilities for job shops and voluntary work opportunities. Courses and faculties often have responsibility for programme-related opportunities. Student Services or Careers services increasingly run student employment bureaux and liaise with the external agencies that operate schemes like STEP and national co-ordination is enhanced by groups such as AGCAS Student Employment Services Working Party.

Student expectations

There is an indication that students may want more from a work experience opportunity than they can reasonably expect (Stone, 1997).

> I had a student who wanted to work on some of the big audio production equipment. Fine, but the reality is that if somebody has a £100,000 bit of kit, they are not going to let you get your hands on it, it's just not going to happen.
>
> (Kemp, 1997)

Students may want to undertake their work experience with a large multi-national organisation because it looks good on the *curriculum vitae* and they are likely to be paid more. However, SMEs may be able to provide a wider range of opportunities to develop the skills required in tomorrow's workplace. On the other hand, SMEs have a greater need to develop the structures to support the learner in the workplace.

Undergraduates are already working part-time during term time to survive. There is considerable potential, with appropriate intervention, to capture, assess and award academic credit for the learning that is gained in such circumstances (Chapter 5).

Creating opportunities

This all begs the question of how real, or how big, is the gap between supply and demand for work experience opportunities. Is it merely a question of investing resources to improve a service, or even to recognise and legitimate existing extracurricular activities?

When it comes to creating opportunities the link tutor has a crucial role to play in managing relationships with other stakeholders. Opportunities most often come about through personal contacts and ex-students often keep in contact with the link tutors and opportunities often arise through this ongoing relationship.

Often companies prefer the students themselves to approach them and organise their own experience. In these instances the link tutor's role is to provide the student with the necessary resources and support.

In many cases, experiences 'roll over' from one year to another which means that institutions are not necessarily looking for *new* opportunities every year. Research carried out at Nottingham Trent University found that 52% of placements were repeated each year and almost half were local to the university (Yarwood, 1997). However, this does not mean that employers who provide opportunities year after year should be taken for granted, they may be put off by an unprofessional approach. Opportunities, it seems, may be won or lost, according to the quality of the service provided by the higher education institution and one bad experience may determine policy for many years to come:

> We did take a placement and it was a very sad experience. I think that the qualification that the person was being offered was reasonable, but I have to be honest and say, obviously, the college got paid to have this person, and the best thing that they could do was dump them on us for five days a week, take the money and run. The level of supervision was atrocious, I thought that it was particularly bad in terms of the student, because the student really thought that they were getting involved in something worthwhile. Here is my favourite example. Part of the NVQ Level 5 in Management and Business Administration was to identify a need within the organisation, examine various options for meeting that need and propose one, showing cost-benefit analysis. This person said, 'Your *photocopier's* not very good, I will go out and price up a few other ones and recommend one to you'. I said that the piece of work was not acceptable, as I would expect that to be done by a clerical grade person, but the college accepted it. That gave me a very good indication of where they were going, they were not interested, and I wouldn't do it again, I wouldn't accept another placement.
>
> (General Manager, small registered charity)

The provision of opportunities for work experience can be seen as one of *many* ways in which higher education institutions link with industry, commerce and the public sector. It is through such liaison that new opportunities are discovered or created.

> …we have a very wide range of courses and we have the opportunity to match students' skills quite carefully to what employers want. But it is very time consuming, and it is a matter of how much resource you can afford to put into giving staff time to talk to employers about what their requirements are.
>
> (Lee, 1997)

Business Bridge, Merseyside is just one example of what is happening in the regions to act as an agency to matching SMEs and skilled students who carry out projects. The approach is flexible in the sense that there is no set length of project and it can be undertaken on a full- or part-time basis.

One of the main objectives of the project is to increase the awareness of SMEs of the potential value of students' contributions to the business. One of the ways in which Business Bridge has achieved this is to provide clear information to overcome the lack of knowledge in this area. Once employers have clear information, they talk to other employers and 'spread the word' about the benefits (Lee, 1997).

The research has identified a number of cases in which finding work experience opportunities for students has not been a problem as long as the resources are there to support the staff to manage the operation. However, there is an increase in demand, especially for well-paid opportunities that occur, mainly in large organisations.

Recommendations

The research into work experience undertaken by the Centre for Research into Quality raises a series of issues that lead to important and wide-ranging recommendations affecting all the key stakeholders: employers, students, staff in higher education institutions, institutional managers, broker agencies and government. The recommendations are designed to:

- increase awareness of the range and benefits of work experience;
- increase the amount of available work experience opportunities;
- enhance the quality of work-experience opportunities;
- encourage further dialogue and links between higher education institutions and employers at local, regional and national levels;
- inform strategic policy decisions.

Employers

Employers are seeking to employ graduates who have commercial awareness and have been exposed to work place cultures. In order to achieve that aim, employers generally should endeavour to *offer more and varied undergraduate work experience opportunities*. In addition, employers should:

- be aware that students are a resource and there is much to gain, for employers of all types and sizes, in providing students with work-experience opportunities. They should be pro-active in linking with higher education institutions and larger employers;
- be aware that work experience takes a variety of forms, and identify which might be most appropriate to them;
- recognise the value of work experience as an integral part of their graduate recruitment strategy;
- look beyond the 'financial bottom line' and have a longer-term vision of the many benefits of providing work experience opportunities for students;
- be aware that providing work experience opportunities helps to develop a learning culture in their organisation;

- recognise the potential of employing students in terms of helping their existing workforce to develop skills for the future;
- maximise the potential of part-time, student employees by utilising them more fully, helping students to recognise the learning; and making links with higher education institutions to help develop a learning culture;
- encourage other organisations with which they are involved, such as supply chains, to offer work experience opportunities;
- recognise the wide range of undergraduates and not just offer opportunities to 'traditional' young, full-time undergraduates;
- recognise that today's students are tomorrow's potentially influential customers;
- not assume that work experience students constitute a 'nuisance' nor confuse work experience for undergraduates with work experience for school children;
- avoid exploitative practices when offering work-experience opportunities.

Students

Students should be aware that *academic prowess alone is insufficient for a successful career* in most fields. In addition, students should:

- recognise the potential for developing a range of skills, attitudes and abilities that come from work experience;
- accept their role as a participant in a learning process and take responsibility for their learning whilst undertaking work experience;
- learn to articulate and understand objectives, anticipate the outcomes and reflect on work experience of all kinds;
- make an active contribution to the organisation providing the work-experience opportunity;
- recognise that there are a range of work-experience options available, which provide different developmental or transformative opportunities that fit into a spectrum of learning;
- aim to develop a portfolio of work experiences;
- bear in mind, when choosing a programme of study, what it is they want to do after graduation;
- be pro-active in arrangements to ensure the quality of the work experience, including preparing for work experience, specifying intended learning outcomes and identifying ways of reflecting on the process;
- be aware that SMEs can often offer a wider range of opportunities for skills development.

Staff in higher education institutions

Staff in higher education institutions should endeavour to develop a wider view of learning (rather than teaching) and *accept that learning also takes place outside the formal academic setting*. In addition, they should:

- value work experience as a significant element of student learning and help students discover how they learn via work experience;
- help students to develop the language to describe their skills and abilities;
- recognise the importance of all types of work experience in the career education and planning process and acknowledge the development of generic skills as well as subject-specific attributes;
- make more effort to develop work-experience contacts with SMEs and the not-for-profit sector and persuade them of the benefits;
- recognise that growing numbers of students have to work part-time during term time to survive, attempt to identify the extent of such work and encourage and enable students to identify and reflect on the learning that comes from it;

- seek ways of linking work experience to the assessment process to optimise the learning that comes from it, especially as assessment is a major factor in helping to shape the way students learn;

- develop more flexible course programmes that allow students to take up project-linked work-experience opportunities throughout the academic year;

- monitor the quality of the learning in the workplace, in particular ensure that expectations are explicit and that all parties are clear about the aims of the experience and their responsibilities – making use of learning contracts where possible;

- ensure that appropriate orientation and training is given to students to prepare them prior to the work experience, facilitate meetings between employers, students and staff at appropriate points during the work experience and act expeditiously to ensure that any problems that arise from work-experience settings are dealt with promptly;

- facilitate a qualitative evaluation by employers and students of the work experience through an accessible and robust debriefing and feedback process and use feedback to improve both the experience and the programme of study to which it relates;

- resist pressure from their institution to cut corners in the placement management process and pursue vigorously the issue of the appropriate funding of work experience;

- network with others in their institution and be willing to share their experiences, contacts and good practice.

Higher education institutions

Senior managers in higher education institutions should endeavour to *do all they can to help their graduates make the transition to the world of work as smooth as possible* by providing a wide range of work-experience opportunities. In particular, they should:

- ensure that funding coming into the institution linked to work experience is not diverted to other activities;

- give academic staff the time and resources to interact with the relevant industrial, commercial or public sector employers to enable them to increase their contacts and capitalise on their knowledge of the field to create work-experience opportunities for their undergraduates;

- give status and provide promotion opportunities to staff who undertake to organise and develop work-experience opportunities for their undergraduates;

- encourage a professional approach to the management of work-experience opportunities;

- arrange for an easily identifiable contact point for employers contacting the institution, which might include a one-stop shop that co-ordinates a range of work experience, a single co-ordinator who co-ordinates faculty-based groups, or a single co-ordinator who can direct organisations to contacts across the university;

- identify and support training needs;

- ensure university-wide procedures and regulations to enable a more flexible incorporation of work-experience opportunities into programmes of study;

- recognise the role played by higher education careers services in identifying potential work experience, disseminating information about opportunities, alerting students to the importance of work experience and advising them about their applications;

- recognise the vital role of work experience in students' career education and planning;

- ensure a commitment at all levels for work experience, backed up by resources;

- be aware of the potential of work experience as a means of extending higher education-employer contacts at both the department and university level;

- ensure clear lines of communication within the institution and with employers about work-experience opportunities and practices.

Broker agencies

Broker agencies (such as STEP, Business Bridge, Placement for Profit, Graduate Link and TECs) should endeavour to *co-operate with higher education institutions to help develop work experience opportunities*. In addition they should:

- make more effort to develop work experience contacts with SMEs and persuade them of the benefits: broker agencies with a business-development brief may be an effective way of contacting SMEs and using marketing initiatives to create a demand within the sector for short, cost-effective project completion by undergraduates;

- enable students to reflect on and learn from work experience of all kinds and help them to develop the language to describe their skills and abilities;

- ensure that students are fully debriefed at the end of periods of work experience or completion of projects;

- nurture any scheme that is running successfully: problems that arise should be dealt with immediately to avoid damage to the reputation of the scheme, particularly amongst employers;

- ensure that students are carefully matched to projects, and that comprehensive orientation training is given to prepare them prior to the work experience;

- ensure that projects are defined carefully at the initial planning stage, and that all parties are clear about their responsibilities;

- monitor the quality of the learning in the workplace and share good practice;

- find ways of complimenting or rewarding good practice;

- facilitate a qualitative evaluation by employers and students of the work experience through an accessible and robust feedback process;

- use feedback from students and employers to improve the experience;

- find ways to accredit work experience.

Government

The Government should endeavour to *use all means at their disposal to encourage the growth of work experience opportunities*. In particular they should:

- carefully monitor the impact of the new funding arrangements, including the introduction of fees, on the opportunities for students' work experience especially formal placements and periods of work experience abroad;

- recognise the important role played by work experience in the development of students' employability skills and in the overall career education and planning process;

- recognise that work experience can make a substantial contribution to student learning and should consider rewarding good practice;

- reward employers for participating in work experience activities by tax incentives;

- encourage the relevant funding agencies to recognise the importance of work experience but also the institutional costs involved in initiating and supporting quality experiences;

- provide funding for institutions to establish and monitor work experience opportunities;

- encourage the Quality Assurance Agency to audit the use of funding provided to establish and monitor work-experience opportunities.

References

Association for Sandwich Education and Training (ASET), 1996, *Directory of Sandwich Courses*. Sheffield, ASET.

Association Internationale des Étudiants en Sciences et Commerciales (AIESEC), 1998, 'The AIESEC Tracker', unpublished.

Association of Graduate Recruiters (AGR) Executive, 1997, Discussion focus group at the AGR Executive Committee Meeting, 15 January, 1997.

Baines, L., 1997, Interview with Ms. Liz Baines, Aston University.

Banta, T. *et al.*, 1991, 'Critique of a method for surveying employers', paper to the 31st Association for Institutional Research (AIR) Annual Forum, San Francisco, 26–29 May, 1991.

Berkeley, J., 1997, Keynote presentation at the Association of Graduate Recruiters' Annual Conference, Warwick University, 7–9 July.

Brennan, J. and Little, B., 1996, *A Review of Work-based Learning in Higher Education*. London, Quality Support Centre.

Brewer, M., 1997a, 'The Dearing Report: ASET's response', *ASET Newsletter*, Issue 18, November.

Brewer, M., 1997b, 'Good practice, necessary practice' in the *ASET Annual Conference: Summary*. Sheffeld, ASET, pp. 32–3.

Brown, S. and Knight, P., 1994, *Assessing Learners in Higher Education*. London, Kogan Page.

Buckingham-Hatfield, S., n.d., *A Learning Partnership for the 1990s*. London, Community Service Volunteers.

Careers Research and Advisory Centre (CRAC), 1996, *Casebook 1997: Placement*. London, Hobsons.

Centre for Research into Quality (CRQ), 1997, *Survey of Sandwich Placement Students*, unpublished report.

Challis, M., 1997, Interview with Ms. Maggie Challis, Sheffield Hallam University. (Now at the University of Nottingham).

Clarke, C., 1997, Letter circulated to Vice-Chancellors and Principals of Higher Education Institutions in England, 18 November, 1997. London, Department for Education and Employment.

Cook, J., 1997, Interview with Ms. Jo Cook, Guinness plc.

Cox, D., 1997, Interview with David Cox, University of Warwick.

CSU-AGCAS-IER, 1996, *Great Expectations: The new diversity of graduate skills and aspirations*. A study undertaken by Purcell, K. and Pitcher, J. of the Institute of Employment Research, University of Warwick on behalf of the Association of Graduate Careers Advisory Services (AGCAS) and Higher Education Careers Services Unit (CSU), October. Manchester, CSU.

Cullen, F., 1998, *STEP Exit Questionnaire Report*, January, unpublished paper.

Cunningham, L., 1997, 'Striding towards capability with STEP', *Capability Journal of Autonomous Learning for Life and Work*, 3(1).

Davies, F., 1997, Keynote presentation at the ASET Annual Conference, University of York, 7–9 April.

Davies, L., 1990, *Experience-Based Learning Within the Curriculum: A synthesis study.* London, Association for Sandwich Education and Training (ASET) and Council for National Academic Awards (CNAA).

Department for Education and Employment (DfEE), 1997, *...working and learning together...: how to get the best out of work-based learning.* Booklet prepared for DfEE by Biggs, C. and Yates, J., edited by Pierce, D. Sheffield, DfEE.

Department for Education and Employment, 1998, 'Higher education and employment: "Graduate Apprenticeships"', National Training Organisation Division, unpublished.

Duckenfield, M. and Stirner, P., 1992, *Higher Education Developments: Learning through work.* Sheffield, Employment Department.

Durkan, C., 1997, Interview with Ms. Caroline Durkan, Glasgow Development Agency.

Edmunds, M., Carter, P. and Lindsay, S., 1997, *The Accreditation of Competence for Sandwich Year Students.* The Executive Summary of a DfEE funded Project in the School of Business and Management at the University of Greenwich.

Edmundson, T. and Carpenter, C., 1994, *University of Westminster Students' Financial Circumstances Report 1994.* London, University of Westminster.

Elton, L., 1993, 'Enterprise in higher education: an agent for change', in Knight, P. T., (ed.) 1994, *University-Wide Change, Staff and Curriculum Development, Staff and Educational Development Association*, SEDA Paper, 83, May 1994, pp. 7–14.

Employment Department Group (EDG), Training Enterprise and Education Directorate, 1991, *Enterprise in Higher Education: Key Features of Enterprise in Higher Education, 1990–91.* Sheffield, Employment Department Group.

Evans, J., 1997, 'After Dearing: Why does work-readiness matter?', keynote presentation by Professor David Watson, Director, the University of Brighton and Judith Evans, Director, Human Resources Policy, Sainsbury's Supermarkets Limited, at the CRAC 'Bridging the Work-Readiness Gap' Conference, 6 November, IBM, South Bank, London.

Ford, J., Bosworth, D. and Wilson, R., 1995, 'Part-time work and full-time higher education', *Studies in Higher Education*, 20(2), pp. 187–202.

Great Britain Committee on Higher Education (GBCHE), 1963, *Higher Education Report of the Committee Appointed by the Prime Minister under the Chairmanship of Lord Robbins, 1961–3.* London, HMSO.

Hallowell, S., 1995, *Student Finance Survey 1994/5.* Leicester, Leicester University.

Hansen, R., 1991, 'The congruence between industry demand and professional school response in architecture', paper to Annual Meeting of the American Educational Research Association, Chicago, April, 1991.

Harvey, L. and Mason, S., 1995, *The Role of Professional Bodies in Quality Monitoring.* Birmingham, QHE.

Harvey, L. with Green, D., 1994, *Employer Satisfaction.* Birmingham, QHE.

Harvey, Moon and Geall, 1997, *Graduates Work: Organisational change and students' attributes.* Birmingham, Centre for Research into Quality (CRQ) and Association of Graduate Recruiters (AGR).

Her Majesty's Inspectorate (HMI), 1993, *A Survey of the Enterprise in Higher Education Initiative in Fifteen Polytechnic and Colleges of Higher Education*, September 1989–March 1991. London, Department for Education (DFE).

Highton, M., 1997, Interview with Ms. Melissa Highton, Napier University.

Hodgson, I., 1997, 'Do cultural differences affect student placements', *ASET Newsletter*, Issue 18, November.

Horn, P., 1997, 'Shopping for skills: how building up points can enhance employability', paper presented at the CRAC 'Bridging the Work-Readiness Gap' Conference, 6 November, IBM, South Bank, London.

Jackson, H., 1997, Interview with Professor Howard Jackson, University of Central England.

Jardine, S.A. and Earl, S.E., 1997, *Academic Industrial Liaison Project. Final Report.* Aberdeen, The Robert Gordon University.

Jones, B., Hunter Jones, J. and Callander, M., 1996, *The Role of Industrial Vocational Experience in Leisure Management Undergraduate Degrees in the United Kingdom, with an Evaluation of the Experience on the Leisure Management Degree at Manchester University*. Manchester, University of Manchester.

Kane, S.T. *et al.*, 1992, 'College students and their part-time jobs: congruency, satisfaction, and quality', *Journal of Employment Counselling*, 29(3), pp. 138–44.

Kemp, D., 1997, Interview with Ms. Diane Kemp, University of Central England.

Knapper, C.K. and Cropley, A.J., 1985, *Lifelong Learning and Higher Education*. London, Croom Helm.

Lee, B., 1997, Interview with Professor Barry Lee, University of Huddersfield.

Leonard, M., 1994, 'Poverty, debt and term-time employment: the reality of student life', paper presented to the Society for Research into Higher Education (SRHE) Annual Conference on 'The Student Experience', 19–21 December, University of York.

Little, B., 1997, 'How can employers help higher education assess key skills?', paper presented at the CRAC 'Bridging the Work-Readiness Gap' Conference, 6 November, IBM, South Bank, London.

MacLeod, L., 1997, Interview with Ms. Lucy MacLeod, Napier University.

Marshall, I., 1997, Interview with Mr. Iain Marshall, Napier University.

Marshall, K., 1997, Interview with Dr. Ken Marshall, formerly of Birmingham TEC.

Mason, G., 1996, *Chemistry Education in a Changing World: Employers' survey*. National Institute of Economic and Social Research (NIESR), mimeo.

Mason, S. and Harvey, L., 1995, *Funding Higher Education: Student perspectives*. Birmingham, Centre for Research into Quality, University of Central England in Birmingham.

Milligan, A., 1997, Interview with Ms. Anne Milligan, Aston University.

Morley, C., 1997, Interview with Ms. Candy Morley, Oxford Brookes University.

Naish, J., 1997, Interview with Ms. Jenny Naish, Middlesex University.

National Committee of Inquiry into Higher Education (NCIHE), 1997, *Higher Education in the Learning Society*. London, HMSO.

Oxford Brookes University School of Hotel and Restaurant Management (OBUSHRM), June 1997, *Employers Guide to the Supervised Work Experience Year*. Oxford, Oxford Brookes University.

Paddon-Smith, M., 1997, Interview with Ms. Maggon Paddon-Smith, Middlesex University.

Paton-Saltzberg, R. and Lindsay, R.O., 1993, *The Effects of Paid Employment on the Academic Performance of Full-time Students in Higher Education*. A report of a study commissioned by the Academic Standards Committee of Oxford Brookes University. Oxford, Oxford Brookes University.

Producers Alliance for Cinema and Television (PACT), 1996, *A Voluntary Code of Practice for Training and Work Experience in the Production Sector*. London, PACT.

Quality Support Centre (QSC), 1996, *Signposts for Staff Development (1)*. London, QSC.

Research into Sandwich Education Committee (RISE), 1985, *An Assessment of the Costs and Benefits of Sandwich Education*. London, Department of Education and Science (DES).

Rover Group, 1998, *Young People Development Survey*, 1997, unpublished report.

Shell Technology Enterprise Programme (STEP), nd, *The Placement Management Handbook: Employers and undergraduates working together*. London, STEP.

Spencer, T., 1997, Interview with Mr. Tom Spencer, University College of Ripon and York St John.

Stewart, S. and Macleod, L., 1997, *Student Teamworking: Involving employers*. LANDSKAPE (Learning and Skills Achievement Through Partnership With Employers). Edinburgh, Napier University.

Stone, G., 1997, Interview with Mr. George Stone, University of the West of England.

Tavistock Institute of Human Relations (TIHR), 1990, *The First Year of Enterprise in Higher Education. Final Report of the Case Study Evaluation of EHE*. Sheffield, Employment Department Group.

The Times Higher Education Supplement (THES), 1998, 'Part-time working 'can harm studies'', 23 January, 1998.

Thorn, S., 1997, Interview with Ms. Sue Thorn, University of Central England.

Tough, A., 1971, *The Adults Learning Projects*. Toronto, Ontario Institute for Studies in Education.

University of Derby, 1997, *The Inside Story, Exposure*. Derby, University of Derby.

Wagner, L., 1997, Keynote presentation at the ASET Annual Conference, University of York, 7–9 April, 1997, in the *ASET Annual Conference: Summary*. Sheffield, ASET, pp. 1–7.

Walkling, P., 1996, Interview with Professor Phil Walkling, University of Central England.

Wallis, M., 1997, 'Work experience available from higher education', paper for the Council for Industry and Higher Education (CIHE), unpublished report.

Watts, A.G., 1997, *Strategic Directions for Careers Services in Higher Education*, Cambridge, NICEC.

Weber, M., 1969, *The Methodology of the Social Sciences*. New York, Free Press.

West Midlands Area National Union of Students (WMNUS), 1997, 'No to tuition fees', leaflet. Birmingham, WMNUS.

Wickenden, D., 1997, Interview with Mr. David Wickenden, People in Business.

Williams, H. and Owen, G., October 1997, *Recruitment and Utilisation of Graduates by Small and Medium Sized Enterprises*. Policy Research Unit, Sheffield Hallam. Departtment for Education and Employment (DfEE) Research Brief.

Wood, J., 1997, 'Developing key skills through the accreditation of work-based learning (undergraduate tutoring in schools)', paper presented at Higher Education for Capability Conference, *Key Skills in Higher Education: Identification, delivery and assessment*, University of London, 21 April, 1997.

Wright, P., 1992, 'Learning through Enterprise: the EHE initiative' in Higher Education Quality Council (HEQC), 1992, *Learning to Effect*. London, HEQC.

Yarwood, C., 1997, 'Obtaining placements' in the *ASET Annual Conference: Summary*. Sheffeld, ASET, pp. 27–8.

Appendix 1   Varieties of work experience

Undergraduate work experience (and experience relevant to work) as part of a programme of study

1   Sandwich course

Sandwich courses usually involve the third year of a four-year degree spent working in industrial, commercial or public-sector organisations with the objective of providing the student with 'relevant' work experience. Students are immersed in the culture and have an opportunity to put some of the academic work into practice in a 'real world' setting. The Association for Sandwich Education and Training (ASET) estimate that 50,000 students are at any time out on a sandwich placement within industry.

The majority of sandwich placements are paid, and ASET estimate that, on average, students in 1997 earned £9,000–£10,000 for a 48-week placement. In limited circumstances programmes provide unpaid placements and students remain in receipt of a grant. In some, relatively rare, circumstances the student is sponsored throughout the course by an employer, and takes the placement year with the employer, and may have worked with that employer for a period of time prior to the commencement of the sponsored full-time course. Final-year sponsorship is also possible in the wake of a satisfactory placement. Sainsbury's, for example, offer one-year placements during which students are assessed and, if successful, may be offered sponsorship in their final year and a permanent job after graduation.

Placements are an integral part of sandwich courses and are usually assessed in some way. At the very least students have to 'successfully complete' the placement to the satisfaction of an academic supervisor who usually takes into account the views of the workplace supervisor. Often there is additional assessment of required written work during the placement year.

Increasingly there is an informal expectation that the student explicitly identifies and reflects on the attributes that have been developed as a result of the work experience. There is usually a de-briefing to help this reflection. The work-based placement supervisor's reference is often an important addendum to the students *curriculum vitae*.

There are over 1000 designated sandwich courses in over 60 universities and they occur in the areas of Built Environment, Business and Management, Engineering and Technology, Maths and Computing, Science, Social Sciences and Hospitality Management. (See Chapter 3 for a discussion of sandwich placements as one form of course-embedded work experience).

2   Professional experience

Professional placements involve a period working in a professional setting, usually as prescribed by professional or regulatory bodies. The objective is for the student to develop competence in the professional area of study. The majority of undergraduate degree programmes related to professional practice involve periods of work experience, including: medicine, nursing, physiotherapy, occupational therapy, radiography, speech therapy, social work, teacher training. Placements on professional courses alternate periods of study with work experience. For example, social work degree courses typically include 55 days placement in the first year and 80 days placement in the third year.

Professional placements are mostly unpaid, with students continuing to receive their grant during the placement. On nursing degrees, where practice placement is a major element of the education, students are paid a bursary, which the higher education institution administers as part of the contract with the regional health authority.

Substantial numbers of students are involved in professional placements, given the link to professional qualifications. In some areas, such as nursing, students provide invaluable additional staffing.

Students usually have to 'successfully complete' the placement period as judged by workplace, professionally qualified (and formally recognised) supervisor(s) in conjunction with the academic supervisor. Assessment may include formal acknowledgement of the acquisition of specified competencies.

3   Work-experience element

There appear to be growing numbers of programmes that provide opportunities for students to spend a period of time in a workplace setting as a structured, assessed and accredited part of the course.

The objective is to develop the subject in a 'real' work setting or to develop employability skills and experience, or a mixture of both. The work experience may be in the private, public or voluntary sector. It is unpaid and ranges from a 4-week block to a whole semester. It is usually a voluntary element of a course, or an optional module. Typically BA Media Studies courses have two 4-week placements at the end of first and second years.

In some cases the work experience element, although part of the programme, takes place during the vacation. For example, BSc Computer Science at the University of Glasgow has a 10-week placement in the summer vacation between the third and fourth years.

An alternative form of embedded work experience is through Graduate Apprenticeships, which are currently being developed for both undergraduates and postgraduates. They will integrate an academic qualification, work experience and accredited key skills. For undergraduates, this could be through an existing HND or degree, or a new course might be devised. Potential benefits include: the student enjoying employed status throughout their study; employers paying the university's costs; the graduates emerging with an academic and an apprenticeship qualification representing a mix of understanding and applied skills (DfEE, 1998).

Short periods of embedded work experience, where students are familiarising themselves with a particular industry are usually not heavily assessed. Where the work experience is an optional module (or substituting for a whole semester's modules) then assessment is often extensive, in order to give it the same weight as students who have taken the standard academic route.

Irrespective of the amount of assessed work, there is usually very little attempt to formally evaluate the effectiveness of the work experience. Although there is growing encouragement for students to make the most of the work experience to develop employability skills, there tends to be little explicit self-reflection on the part of the student. However, some programmes do require that the student keeps a learning log, reflecting on the development of skills, which is used as a significant part of the assessment.

Undergraduate courses in recreation management, tourism, sports studies, media studies have this type of work experience, but it is also beginning to appear in other areas. For example, BA Sociology at UCE has a one semester, nominally optional, work-experience element as part of the programme of study, equivalent to five modules, in which the student works in an organisation undertaking work that is related in some way to the discipline subject area. The work experience is heavily assessed towards the final award. Students are usually unpaid and in receipt of a grant or loan.

The main issue is how to assess the experience as part of the assessment towards the degree. Should it be full-time (to simulate a working situation) or could it be undertaken on a part-time basis (allowing for academic modules to be taken simultaneously)? If full-time, then must it be for a full semester, or are organisational arrangements flexible enough to accommodate fractions of a semester? If for a full semester, there are assessment implications, as it needs to be 'equivalent' to half a year's worth of modules, an issue that is particularly acute where the work-experience element is optional. (Work-experience elements are discussed further in Chapter 3).

4 Overseas work-experience placement

Some courses make provision for overseas placement in a structured work-experience situation. These are distinct from the year spent overseas, by language students, in a foreign university. For example, Aston University's language sandwich students have the opportunity to spend their sandwich year either on an exchange with a foreign university, as a language assistant in schools or on an industrial placement.

These overseas work-experience placements are usually in other European countries, offered by a range of commercial, industrial and public sector organisations. They are intended to widen the experience and cultural appreciation of students as well as develop employability skills. Typically, they last from 3 to 6 months although shorter or longer periods occur. They involve a relatively small proportion of students and are often poorly paid. The principal European schemes are Stage (France) and Praktikum (Germany).

The *European Commission (EC)* organises in-service training periods in Brussels, twice a year. Each 'stage' lasts between 3 and 5 months. The aim of the project is to give trainees a general idea about objectives of and issues relating to European integration and to give practical knowledge of the working of Commission departments. They offer around 700 places and 400 of these are funded. Trainees need to be able to financially support their living costs (Brussels is an expensive city).

The *Leonardo da Vinci* programme, funded by the European Community, also provides opportunities for industrial training in Europe for undergraduates and recent graduates for periods of between 3 and 12 months. The programme does not pay a salary, that is for the student to negotiate with their employer. Leonardo can make a contribution towards language tuition and travel costs. Placements are integrated within the student's academic programme. It accounts for about 20% of European placements.

5 Work-linked individual project

Some programmes have provision for students to undertake an individual project linked to a workplace. The student uses the workplace resources or setting to undertake an enquiry, or is actively engaged in an employer-generated project. This may be solving a problem, establishing a system, writing a manual, and so on. Many sandwich placement students also produce projects for assessment, based on their year's experience, but this category is intended to refer to students who produce a work-linked project outside any formal placement situation. This category requires some time on the employer site working on a specific project. For example, students on many Business Studies degrees undertake an action-learning project that provides consultancy for an employer for little or no direct cost, but may require some initial set-up time and involvement on the part of the employer organisation.

The objectives are to provide an opportunity to develop the subject, and appreciate constraints in a 'real' work setting. It is expected that a specific problem will be investigated and, preferably, solved.

Projects are usually for between 6 and 8 weeks, but may be for a whole semester of 15 weeks and exceptionally for half a year. The Glasgow-based Profit by Placement Scheme offers project-based, work-experience opportunities that are planned to run alongside other units of the course for up to 26 weeks. Sometimes it is the sole course element for those weeks, although often undertaken as one unit or module in parallel with other units.

Work-linked individual projects are usually a voluntary element of a course and at undergraduate level is unpaid. Usually, the experience is linked to producing a written project or extended essay for assessment purposes. There may be an oral report element to the assessment. Sometimes the project might be submitted in other media, such as video, or the outcome may be produced specifically for the organisation and assessment would be based on whether it fulfils expectations.

Evaluation of the value of the experience is rare. There is often an implicit assumption that value is coterminous with the quality of the outcome. (Work-linked projects are discussed further in Chapter 4.)

6   Work-linked group project

A group project, linked to a workplace, involves similar arrangements to the individual project. A group or team of students uses the workplace resources or setting to undertake an enquiry or is actively engaged in an employer-generated project. Again this may be solving a problem, establishing a system, writing a manual, or undertaking a small research study. For example, the LANDSKAPE project at Napier involves 'live' projects based on real needs identified by outside employing organisations and the use of real-life problem-solving exercises in the curriculum. Similarly, students on BA Planning (UCE) work in multidisciplinary teams on a client-based project.

The objectives are to provide students with the opportunity to work in a team to develop the subject and appreciate constraints in a 'real' work setting. For example, at Central Saint Martins College of Art and Design, part of the London Institute, course projects are planned with outside organisations, for example theatre designers worked with the English National Ballet for four new dance works and ceramic designers worked with Conran contracts to design tableware for a new 1000 seat restaurant in Soho.

Projects are usually for 6 to 8 weeks but may be for a semester. (Unusually, the Glasgow Profit by Placement Project plans to facilitate group projects for up to 32 weeks). Occasionally, the group project is the sole course element for those weeks, but more often is undertaken as one unit in parallel with other units. It is usually a voluntary, unpaid element of a course. There are not very many students involved in this but it is an area that appears to be growing slowly.

Only the outcome of the work, in the form of a team-written academic project or dissertation, tends to be assessed. There is rarely any attempt to assess team working *per se*. Sometimes the project might be submitted in other media, such as video, or may be aimed at the organisation and take the form of a ('non-academic') report with recommendations or the setting up of a database or set of procedures. There is often a group oral report element to the assessment. (Work-linked projects are discussed further in Chapter 4.)

7 Workplace visit

This is a short visit to a work environment arranged as part of a programme of study. Workplace visits are reasonably widespread in 'vocational' areas. They provide career tasters and raise student awareness of a course-related workplace. They are usually a day or half a day visits with no assessment attached and take place in the local region. Evaluation of the experience tends to be very limited, possibly a classroom discussion of what was learned from the visit.

8 Simulated case studies

Simulated case studies attempt to replicate the learning that derives from work experience without the student, or group of students, working in an employer organisation. Leeds University is developing a series of work-experience simulations in a variety of academic departments. Eventually this system could be used in other institutions too.

Organised experience relevant to work, external to the programme of study

9 Structured vacation work programme

Students apply for, and are selected to work on, an organised programme that offers students a period of project-linked, structured work experience during the vacation. The objective is for students to obtain 'relevant' experience and insight. The work is usually directly linked to employability skills and often to a related subject area.

The Shell STEP scheme is probably the best-known example. It involves an eight-week project in an SME. It gives experience of the business and also teaches students about team working, problem solving, communication and decision making. Students give presentations and compete for awards. There is an agency network but it is resource intensive and therefore of restricted scope.

These programmes involve a relatively small proportion of students. 1500 students per year are on Shell STEP. Business Bridge, in Merseyside, for example, offer variable length projects that can be undertaken during term-time or in vacations. There were 375 'bridges' in the first year of the project.

Organised vacation work programmes are usually for up to 10 weeks, based on a standard full-time week's work. Students are normally paid. Shell STEP students are paid £110 per week. Business Bridge recommend students are paid £20 per day by employers. (See Chapter 4 for further discussion of employer-linked, project-based work experience.)

10 Work-experience vacation placement

Various organisations advertise work-experience vacation placements and students apply for them. They provide a taster and are a potential recruitment vehicle. (The number of advertised schemes is a good indicator of the state of the graduate recruitment market). They last from 2 to 12 weeks. Getting on these programmes is often difficult as companies have rigorous selection criteria and may undertake assessment of students during the placement.

Only a small proportion of students are involved in this form of work experience. Subsistence allowance and travel expenses are usually paid and sometimes a salary.

The opportunities are offered by large employers including Civil Service, banks, major retailers, accountancy firms, solicitors, research laboratories, industrial sales and marketing.

For example, Procter and Gamble run a Summer Internship Programme, which involves working in a real business team on projects specifically designed to test the student's ability. They give preference to penultimate year students. Interviews are carried out on a one-to-one basis and if the applicant is successful they attend a three-day introductory course which provides them with essential training, skills and knowledge before they begin the programme. The scheme lasts for up to 12 weeks over the summer holiday and the students earn around £3,000. Sainsbury's operate a Vacation Training Scheme, open to penultimate year students. Students undertake a six-week placement during the summer vacation as trainee store managers. Performance is assessed and this determines whether the student is offered a permanent position. If they are successful, they are sponsored for £1,000 during their final year at university.

11 Organised world-wide placements

Organised world-wide placements are work placements abroad arranged by an international organisation. They are designed to widen experience both of the workplace and of other cultures and languages. Places are limited so relatively few students are involved.

To take advantage of these opportunities students are often required to be members of the campus branch of the organisations. Students are usually paid (although often not very much) but often have to make an initial investment to cover such things as travel costs.

The International Association for the Exchange of Students for Technical Experience (IAESTE) offers science and engineering students paid, course-related training abroad, in one of 63 countries. IAESTE aims to promote international understanding and goodwill amongst students of all nations. In 1994, 2,622 employers participated in the scheme. The training placements last between 8 and 12 weeks during the summer months and firms are expected to pay the student a sufficient wage (to cover living costs). There is a charge of £48 to find a placement and students must pay their travel expenses.

British Universities North America Club (BUNAC) is a non-profit making organisation that runs several schemes during the summer including: Work America, Work Canada, BUNACAMP (British Counselling Placement), KAMP (Kitchen and Maintenance Programme) and Work Australia. Anyone between 18 and 25 can apply, providing they have sufficient funds to cover airfare, insurance, personal support and the programme fee: about £2,000 in all.

L'Association Internationale des Étudiants en Sciences et Commerciales (AIESEC) is a student-run, non-profit making organisation with connections in 85 countries. They offer projects for undergraduates and recent graduates, which aim to put a different perspective on global issues. Each year 8000 undergraduates and graduates travel abroad on this programme. Placements can last from 6 weeks to 18 months.

12 Short vacation courses and periods of induction

There are various 'courses' that provide short periods with a firm or simulated experiences via a specialised agency. They are designed to increase awareness and usually involve a skills training component. They usually last for one to three days. A relatively small proportion of students get involved in this type of activity.

For example, the Careers Research and Advisory Council (CRAC) run an Insight into Management course. It is a programme for managers and potential managers that looks at personal skills and development and at the way business works. It is designed for young managers to develop their skills and share experiences with participants. It helps students with team work, developing skills and enhancing business awareness. For the organisation itself, the course is designed to enhance young managers and to help improve effectiveness at work.

Similarly, the Engineering and Physical Sciences Research Council (EPSRC) Graduate Schools Programme is a personal-development course for science and technology Ph.D. students and new managers. The course lasts for five days and is designed to build on personal skills and help enhance career development. The course focuses on the following skills: planning, problem solving and decision making, communication and negotiation, team working and attributes such as initiative, enthusiasm and self-knowledge.

The Graduate Development Programme is a modular programme for organisations concerned with recruitment and development of graduates. The programme includes self management, business management and team management. The programme uses work-related and activity-based approaches.

The Home Office runs familiarisation courses every year, which offer an opportunity for undergraduates to spend three or four days with the police. They operate in about twenty different locations each year with places for around 500–600 students.

The Price Waterhouse Experience is a three-day placement to market the firm and interest students in information technology and consultancy. The first day is spent at Head Office, which includes being shown around, a presentation and team games. The second and third days take place in a hotel and include consultancy games, a team video-making project and a session on communication skills. They also include tips on recruitment techniques. The scheme is aimed at undergraduates from any discipline, and no previous information-technology knowledge is required.

13 Work shadowing and mentoring

Work shadowing involves formal or informal observation of the work situation. It is often an informal arrangement between student and organisation but some firms have a formal scheme.

The objective is to raise awareness. It provides valuable insights and a mini-career taster and can give a well-rounded view of an organisation in a short time – from one day to a couple of weeks.

A relatively small proportion of students are involved in this kind of experience, which includes informal 'fly-on-the-wall' observation of settings such as social work, journalism, teaching, hospital administration, advertising, media, Civil Service or, more formally, mini-pupillages in barristers' chambers.

For example, Northumberland TEC funded a work-shadowing scheme that allowed 25 second-year students to undertake work shadowing of a graduate-level job for one week in June. The scheme paid for travel costs and some administrative costs. It provided students with information on what they needed to consider during the week of work shadowing. It stressed that they should look at the skills that the people doing the job needed and other things such as career structure and management structures. Typically the jobs were of quite a high level so the week was not boring. One aim was to encourage retention of graduates in the area. Although a positive experience for students who took up the opportunity, the scheme found it very difficult to get the students involved. The main problem was a mismatch between the areas in which students were interested and the local employment sector. The project was far too cost intensive, particularly in terms of liaising with the employer organisations and checking on health and safety and insurance.

The Ethnic Minority Mentoring project at Wolverhampton University is a small programme that has operated since 1995, sub-contracted by the University of East London (UEL) and the National Mentoring Consortium. It is available for 15 students. It is not a validated module and needs to be undertaken in the second or third year. This is aimed specifically at students from ethnic minorities as statistics show these graduates are more likely to be unemployed than white graduates. The aim is to address discrimination in the employment market. UEL supplies a list of major employers with outlets in the region, such as Boots, Customs and Excise, Barclays, BBC. The student has a mentor with whom they liaise over six months to help the self-development of the student, for example, develop a *curriculum vitae*, learn about assessment centres, undertake work shadowing and project work. The scheme has had very positive feedback from students involved in this process. Involvement is seen as a positive experience for the mentors as well as the students. Wolverhampton University funds this centrally, so expansion is restricted to the funds available. At the moment it is an excellent, high quality experience but it is limited to small numbers of participants.

Ad hoc work experience external to the programme of study

14   Traditional vacation work

Traditional vacation work, which students arrange for themselves as a way of earning money out of term time, provides another form of work experience. The job *may* include relevant experience for future intended work. It gives a 'worm's eye view of the company' and can lead to a permanent relationship and maybe permanent work. It is useful on a *curriculum vitae* when applying for jobs after graduation, provided the student is able to reflect on what has been learned from the experience.

Typically students work in a wide variety of jobs in the service sector and, to a lesser extent, manufacturing, especially in seasonal jobs. Some areas, such as Teaching English as a Foreign Language, depend on additional student labour during the Summer.

The majority of students undertake some type of vacation work at some point during their undergraduate study. However, this is often underdeveloped in terms of reflective experience and nowhere, to date, is it incorporated into any formal assessment towards a programme of study. As 'records of achievement' or 'individual profiles' emerge in higher education, some way needs to be developed to incorporate the learning that comes from traditional vacation work (see Chapter 5).

15   Term-time, part-time work

Working in a part-time job, to earn money, during term time is becoming increasingly common with surveys suggesting that 50-60% of full-time students are undertaking term-time, part-time work at any one time. Increasingly there are campus-based 'job shops' helping students find such work.

The kinds of jobs undertaken include, working in supermarkets, fast-food outlets, pubs, night-clubs, as couriers, and so on. They are not always 'formal' jobs and are sometimes paid 'cash-in-hand'. These jobs rarely include directly relevant experience for future-intended work, nor are they often linked very strongly to the subject discipline. They may possibly be an experience to add to the *curriculum vitae* although there is little evidence of much reflection on skills developed during such work. A minority of students are making the most of this work when applying for jobs, by reflecting on the experience, good or bad. The value of such part-time work depends on the motivation and objectives of the individual and the extent to which the employer is aware of them and is prepared to embrace them.

Some institutions are beginning to explore ways of assessing and accrediting this form of work experience. (See Chapter 5 for an extended discussion of term-time, part-time work.)

16   Working in the family business

Working in the family business provides another work experience, often not appreciated by those involved. It includes experiences such as helping on a family farm, working in a family-run restaurant and doing clerical work in the family business. Students involved in this kind of work tend to take it for granted and rarely reflect on it in terms of the development of a range of attributes. It is a greatly underestimated experience and tends not to be regarded as a serious learning situation. The work may be undertaken out of convenience or obligation and may involve payment, although not always in cash terms. The work rarely includes directly relevant experience for future intended work nor is it often linked very strongly to the subject discipline.

17   Voluntary work, term time

Unpaid voluntary work undertaken in term time is another form of work experience. It is usually to gain experience in a 'relevant' area with an eye on a future career, or out of interest or commitment, to broaden experience. It may or may not be linked to the academic subject or be designed to develop 'employability' skills. It is often an experience to add to the student's *curriculum vitae*. In some discipline areas, undertaking this kind of voluntary work can be seen as an advantage when applying for jobs.

A relatively small proportion of students are involved in this kind of work, which includes such things as a law student working in a community-based law centre on a voluntary basis for one day a week and a media student working on a local hospital radio station. Indeed, many student unions have active 'community service' groups. Charities, social services, public relations, newspapers, museums, libraries, church-run holiday activities, political parties and pressure groups all take students as volunteers.

There are some organisations that offer listings of opportunities for a vast range of voluntary work. For example, Youth for Britain aims to make it possible for young people to be involved in voluntary work. They provide information rather than the placement itself. They identify a huge range of volunteering opportunities and include other providers such as GAP and CSV on the database. Youth for Britain can offer about 250,000 opportunities. The opportunities range from a week to a year in length. All are full-time opportunities. A volunteer's requirement is matched with the database. Information from the voluntary organisation includes: contact details, qualifications, costs and benefits, health requirements, accreditation, what they do and a 200–300 word broad description. They can search the database by any relevant variables, such as any UK county or any country. Individuals can contact Youth for Britain directly for a £15 search fee. There are also subscriber organisations, including some student unions, that pay an annual subscription (£95) and get a 6-month update. Future developments might include developing a placement service, like a clearing system, so they could tell what opportunities are actually vacant at any one time. There is also potential to expand outside the UK.

Some institutions are beginning to find ways of accrediting term-time voluntary work as part of the programme, usually by creating specialised optional modules. For example, Napier University accredits two types of voluntary work: working in a voluntary agency or working as voluntary classroom assistants in schools. Students, with previous experience of voluntary work of this kind, may opt to undertake a module linked to a further period of voluntary work, which includes clearly identified assessment criteria. The module is taken in parallel to the required number of other modules for the semester. In a sense, this process is similar to a programme-embedded period of work experience but on a part-time basis, restricted to the voluntary sector. (See Chapter 5 for extended discussion of term-time, part-time work).

Assessment of student tutors has three components: formative logbook (including personal action plan); summative formal written report; summative oral presentation. All procedures and criteria for assessment are made clear in the form of a booklet they receive during their training sessions and at a briefing session part-way through the tutoring. Some student tutoring programmes include an assessment mark given by the teacher. In this project, tutoring is assessed through visits to the placement by project staff and by means of a brief evaluation by the teacher.

There is some concern that crediting voluntary work undermines its integrity: the value of tutoring as a completely extra-curricular activity is diminished if it is credited. Concerns include: the perceptions of extra 'pressure' on the quality of tutoring, considerations of equable assessment and what happens if the placement does not run smoothly.

18 Voluntary work, vacations and after graduation

Voluntary work also takes place during vacations and after graduation. It is usually undertaken to widen horizons but may be linked to a 'relevant' area. Many summer activities such as play schemes rely heavily on voluntary student helpers.

Vacation and post-graduation voluntary work is often of a more organised type than that undertaken in term time. For example, Voluntary Service Overseas (VSO) involves working alongside local people with the aim of sharing expertise in the areas of education, health, natural resources, business and social development. Students need to be over 20 and have a formal qualification. Postings are for two years and volunteers are provided with accommodation and a local level allowance. Air fare and insurance are also provided.

Raleigh International projects are 10-week expeditions abroad on community, environmental and adventure projects. Participants need to be between 17 and 24, have a basic level of fitness and understanding of English. Selection is usually through an assessment weekend, which includes problem solving, team working and provides an insight into expedition life. Volunteers are expected to raise sufficient funds towards the cost of the programme.

Community Service Volunteers (CSV) offer placements in the UK within the local community. Skills, interests and experience are matched to the setting.

Voluntary work during vacations and after graduation might not necessarily involve working in a voluntary organisation, it may be working unpaid in a commercial or public organisation, for example, media students working unpaid in various media organisations to build up a *curriculum vitae* of experience. In some discipline areas, periods of voluntary work can be seen as an advantage when applying for jobs.

Voluntary work is unpaid except, perhaps, for basic overseas travel expenses and subsistence. Some placements will offer board and lodgings and a small salary, whilst for others funds may need to be raised. A relatively small proportion of students are involved in this kind of work.

19 Time off during the programme

Some students take a break in study to undertake a period of work at home or abroad. This may be on student initiative or negotiated between the academic department and the employer. It is usually to broaden experience or alleviate financial hardship, or both. The break in study may be linked to subject discipline and is possibly an experience to add to the student's *curriculum vitae*.

The break is usually an academic or calendar year, so that the student can recommence at the same point on the course. It affects a relatively small, but probably growing, proportion of students. It is possible that some students will take a break in the programme, rather than a sandwich placement year, to avoid paying the £500 fee proposed for sandwich years.

20 Gap year

A 'gap year' involves taking a year (or more) out before or after an undergraduate programme and working in one or more jobs, often while travelling. The objective is to broaden the student's experience and maybe also to earn money. It is usually an experience to add to the student's *curriculum vitae*. Gap years are taken anywhere, but are usually away from home, especially in the case of post-graduation gap years. The number of students doing this is slowly growing.

Gap Activity Projects (GAP) promotes international projects for young people. The emphasis is on voluntary work and there are projects in 33 countries world-wide. It is for volunteers run by volunteers. GAP places roughly 1300 young people per year. GAP placements are unpaid except for subsistence. Volunteers have to pay for administration and registration costs and their air fare. Placements typically last between 6 and 9 months.

Appendix 2   Organisational approach and work experience

The variety of work experience opportunities is paralleled by a range of different perceptions about the efficacy and effectiveness of work experience that relate to the organisational profile of the work experience setting.

In *Graduates' Work*, the idea of a workplace profile was introduced to help understand the relationship between graduate attributes and organisational change (Harvey, Moon and Geall, 1997, p. 31). The profile identified the way that organisations (or parts of organisations) with different priorities related desirable graduate attributes to elements of their organisational structure and practices (Figure A2.1). The profile expanded the enhancement continuum of graduate attributes and approach to work (Figure A2.2), to explore such elements as organisational flexibility and ethos, the nature of employer empowerment, employee loyalty, recruitment practices, staff training and development, and higher education-employer links.

An adaptation of the workplace profile provides a framework for exploring the benefits of *work experience* for organisations, students and academic staff in higher education institutions. Not all students view work experience in the same way. For example, they may see it as providing an opportunity to put knowledge, derived from the programme of study, into practice in the 'real world'. Alternatively, they may see work experience as an opportunity to develop personal attributes, such as self-confidence and time-management. Similarly, employers view work experience in different ways. Some, for example, may welcome the extra pair of hands, others may see it as an opportunity to contribute to the student's education. Staff in higher education institutions, and brokers arranging work-experience opportunities, likewise, may have differing agendas when placing students.

The following analysis outlines the different perspectives under the relevant headings of the workplace profile (Figure A2.3). For the sake of simplicity it points to the opposing ends of the spectrum, suggesting at one end the 'value added' approach and at the other a 'stakeholder approach'. However, it must be borne in mind that the following analysis suggests 'ideal types' (Weber, 1969) rather than rigid specifications. In practice, organisations are not homogeneous, different sections or departments will behave in different ways. Similarly, a nominally 'added-value organisation' in respect of one section of the workplace profile may not follow that route consistently through all elements. So, for example, an organisation (or part of an organisation) may be driven by the financial bottom-line but not simply recruit 'safe' graduates who will fit in.

Ethos

The added-value organisation places emphasis on its 'financial bottom-line' and tends to expect work experience to provide some short-term return for the organisation's investment of time and resources. The student undertaking work experience should actually contribute to the organisation in some way, to an extent that goes beyond the supervisory time, work experience organisational costs and other resource costs that the employer has to meet.

At the other end of the spectrum, the stakeholder organisation, although cost conscious, shifts emphasis away from financial imperatives and adopts a wider range of responses to customers, clients and stakeholders. It has a long-term vision of the benefits of work experience to all parties involved. There is a recognition of the learning that is associated with work experience, not just its immediate benefits in the workplace but for the long-term developments, of the individuals involved and of the developments between higher education and employers.

Figure A2.1   Workplace profile

	Adding value	Evolving	Transforming
Flexible organisation Ethos and performance criteria	Cost-flexible. Short-term investments Success = profit, one-dimensional PI, financial imperatives.	Response flexible. Cost conscious but attempting to develop partnerships with client groups to secure longer-term future.	Stakeholder flexible. Long-term vision – 'inclusive' Multi-layered PIs, socially responsible: stakeholder criteria.
Empowerment	Self-regulatory empowerment	Delegated empowerment	Stakeholder empowerment
Graduate attributes and approach	Adaptive: knowledge and skills brought to the organisation. Ability to fit in to organisational culture. Takes no risks, does job competently. 'Yes' people who have high expectations that if they please others they will succeed.	Adaptable: Ability to learn and add to knowledge and skill, ability to use knowledge and skills in face of change, to interact effectively, work in teams and communicate at a variety of levels. Demonstrates initiative within a pre-set framework.	Transformative: the use of transformative skills (analysis, critique, synthesis, multi-layered communication) to facilitate innovative teamwork. Inventive, knows boundaries but pushes them.
Employee loyalty	Loyalty dependent on cash and promotion.	Loyalty based on perception of future progress and commitment to principles of organisation.	Wider commitment to organisation through direct involvement as acknowledged stakeholder.
Staff development and training	Looking for enhancement of job-related competencies: return on investment.	Broader enhancement of staff, although still circumscribed by job relevance.	Learning organisation. Competencies plus: empower employees through broad development of staff.
Recruitment	Safe, conservative – prioritise those who will fit in.	Mixture of job-specific and speculative recruitment as senior management/ partner feed stock.	Risky – innovative, seeking those who will lead change.
Higher education– Employer interface	Employers as customers interested in value for money. HE as supplier of product, looking for additional cash.	Mutual involvement in mainly short-term projects for added-value.	Employers as participants, interested in spending time and effort as well as cash in building relationships. Academics listening. Development of partner-ship and exchange of ideas.

Source: Harvey, Moon and Geall, 1997, p. 31

Figure A2.2   Enhancement continuum

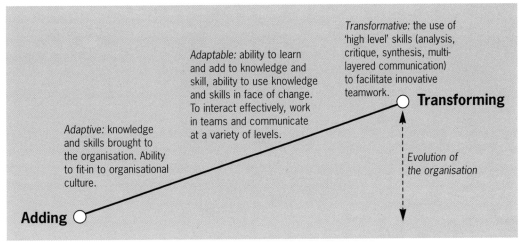

Source: Harvey, Moon and Geall, 1997, p. 22

Students in the added-value organisation get an insight into the pressured world of finance-driven employment, learning the crucial importance of meeting deadlines and being assessed on performance.

In the stakeholder organisation, students get a range of involvement and an insight into organisational cultures. They have the opportunity to develop teamwork, communication and interpersonal skills. However, work-experience students are also regarded as having a valuable input, not just in immediate tasks or contributions within teams but also in pushing the boundaries of the organisation, developing new ideas and taking a leading or inspiring role.

For academic staff within the higher education institution, the focused approach of the added-value organisation provides a potential work location where students may put their subject knowledge into practice. A clearly articulated experience may be specified in a work-experience contract so that both sides are able to monitor 'success'.

On the other hand, the responsive approach of the stakeholder organisation provides a dialogue with employers which can help to explore relationships between subject matter and the real world. It may also lead to an ongoing partnership, which may include employer input into the design and development of the work-experience opportunities or input into the development of the curriculum.

Culture and empowerment

In added-value organisations, students tend to be given specific tasks, a specific job role or projects to complete. Completion of work is clearly a benefit for the employer but it only constitutes an overall gain if the outcome outweighs the time to set up the task or project and the subsequent effort expended in supervision. Value-added organisations tend to have to be convinced that the student does not constitute a 'nuisance' factor to be 'put up with' but a valuable team member to whom tasks or roles may be delegated.

Work-experience students have to rapidly assimilate the organisational culture. Once inducted, they have to be able to undertake tasks with a minimum of ongoing supervision and be able to self-regulate. The development of a general awareness of workplace culture and an appreciation of the work environment broadens students' perceptions and, incidentally, makes them more employable (Harvey, Moon and Geall, 1997). It also provides a useful insight into organisational structure and management (CRAC, 1996). For work-experience students in the 'value-added' setting the demonstration of personal skills such as time-management, organisational awareness, self-discipline, and self-awareness are at a premium.

In stakeholder organisations, students tend to have the autonomy to be able to tackle issues and problems within their framework. This does not mean that there should be no support, rather that it focuses on enabling the student rather than directing. It is more likely that students will be supervised within the context of the team structure and thus, in practice, have different supervisors within different project teams. They would be delegated a considerable degree of responsibility and would be under pressure to perform within that context. Although this greater degree of empowerment provides students with a significant feeling of ownership, it also places considerable pressure on them to deliver within organisational parameters. Probably the hardest aspect of operating as a work-experience student in this situation, is identifying when to seek advice and assistance.

Graduate attributes and approach

Value-added employers are looking for work-experience students who are adaptive: who apply their knowledge and skills to the work situation and competently complete tasks allocated to them (see the enhancement continuum (Figure A2.2)). The opportunity to do this is an invaluable learning experience for students. Academic staff tend to see this as beneficial if it can be linked to subject-discipline knowledge.

The stakeholder organisation, on the other hand, is, ideally, looking for work-experience students who are transformative: who can effectively communicate internally and externally and are able to develop their ideas and convince others through persuasion and negotiation.

Students on work experience in such situations would be expected quickly to develop the ability to interact effectively with a variety of people, work in teams taking a variety of roles, be effective communicators on a range of levels and to be able to work simultaneously on several different projects at once. The work-experience student would be expected to show initiative within clearly defined boundaries.

From the point of the academic staff, a work-experience placement in this setting helps provide not just the opportunity to put subject matter into practice as an incidental part of the everyday operation of the organisation but also positive encouragement to explore the relationship between the subject matter and the everyday reality of the work setting.

Staff development and training

Training, in the value-added setting, will tend to be instrumental, adding only those incremental skills that will enable the student to undertake the required task. The expectation will be that the student will be equipped, usually with an appropriate level of subject knowledge, research skills and general intelligence to be able to operate without much further training. The development of employability skills will tend to be on-the-job acquisition through a rapid assimilation of the way the organisation works.

Training in the stakeholder setting will tend to be holistic rather than task focused. It will tend to be directed more at general development of employability skills within the remit of the work-experience context rather than the incremental development of necessary additional skills required to perform tasks or to be effective in the specific work setting.

The necessary staff development associated with supporting or mentoring students is recognised as a useful staff-development tool by some organisations (CRAC, 1996).

Employer-higher education interface

The work-experience-based link between employers and higher education for the value-added organisation tends to be one of mutual opportunism. The employer wants someone to add value by fitting in or undertaking a specific project and the higher education institution is looking for a situation where the student may put into practice subject-related knowledge and, incidentally, develop employability skills and abilities.

Work-opportunity links between higher education and employers have the potential to be mutually beneficial in the future. For example, employers can influence developments within departments at degree programme level, so helping to tailor their future workforce.

The work-experience-based link between employers and higher education for stakeholder organisations is seen as an opportunity for mutual, forward-looking development.

By providing opportunities for work experience for undergraduates, employers can make and maintain links with individual higher education institutions. This can also be used as a way of enhancing the image of the company through promoting its function as a learning organisation. For example, for some organisations, this was an outcome of their involvement in the Enterprise in Higher Education programme. Links with institutions can also be exploited for other purposes, such as collaborative research.

In the same way that it is important to apply the workplace profile with care, the following points should be borne in mind when making use of the work-experience opportunity profile as an interpretative framework.

- The work-experience opportunity profile is an orienting device to help understand how work experience relates to different kinds of organisational ethos and priorities.

- The profile should not be seen as implying a desirable, optimum or stable state, to which individuals or organisations should strive. The position on the profile will, in part, be determined by external forces. Equally, as is discussed in Chapter 2, there is no 'ideal' model of work experience. It is the learning that derives from the work experience rather than the experience itself that is important.

- There is no assumption that all individuals, or all parts of a complex organisation, will fit into a single point on any dimension of the profile. Some parts of an organisation may need to focus on adding-value while others may prioritise innovation.

Figure A2.3   Work-experience opportunity profile

	Adding value	Transforming
Flexible organisation	Cost-flexible.	Stakeholder flexible.
Ethos and performance criteria	Short-term return, work-experience student contribution expected to exceed costs.	Immediate benefits and value long-term input of developing ideas and progressing the organisation.
Empowerment	Students must rapidly assimilate culture and self-regulate.	More autonomy with focus on enabling rather than directing students.
Graduate attributes and approach	Adaptive: apply knowledge and skills to a project or in a specific role.	Transformative: Communicate effectively internally and externally, develop ideas and convince others.
Staff development and training	Instrumental approach to adding necessary additional skills. On-the-job, incidental acquisition of employability skills.	Learning organisation. Holistic rather than task-focused approach, a general development of employability skills.
Higher education- Employer interface	Mutual opportunism between employer and HEI. Potential for direct impact on HEI study programme. Students may enhance employment prospects with organisation.	Mutual forward-looking development, can promote organisation as a learning organisation, can build on links e.g. collaborative research.

What this schema offers is a means by which to understand the role that work experience plays and the likely benefits that accrue from it in organisations with differing priorities and cultures.

Therefore, the organisations' approaches to the different forms of work experience will span the spectrum suggested in the profile, and one form of work experience is not restricted to any point on the adding value-evolving-transforming continuum. For example, organisational approach to project-based work experience such as Shell STEP may range through projects that are looking for immediate rewards, to projects that want someone to progress ideas, to projects that take the organisation in a new direction with long-term implications.

This spanning of approaches is true of the variety of work experiences, though some may seem to concentrate at particular ends of the spectrum. For example, the approach of organisations employing students part-time may predominately be cost flexible, that is employing them to ensure immediate demands are met. However, there are examples of organisations that have taken on board the development of the student as a learner in these types of jobs (for example, ASDA Flying Start, MacDonalds[1])

---

1   Both approaches were discussed at a 1997 CIHE/CRAC conference, Bridging the Work Readiness GAP, 6/11/97, London, in workshop sessions.

Appendix 3   Participants

Interviews

The following were interviewed by researchers at the Centre for Research into Quality as part of the research.

Ms Liz Baines	School of Languages and European Studies	Aston University
Ms Anne Milligan	Aston Business School	Aston University
Dr Ken Marshall	Higher Education Sector Co-ordinator	Birmingham TEC
Ms Vicky Cartwright	Student Unit	Business Bridge
Ms Alison Thornber	Central Unit	Business Bridge
Mr Geoff Hutt	Centre Manager	Birmingham TCS
Ms Kate Slavin	Contract Manager	ENTRUST
Brigadier John Cornell	Director	GAP
Ms Pamela Williams-Jones	Appeals Director	GAP
Mr Gerald Shaw	Economics Department	Glasgow Caledonian University
Ms Caroline Durkan	Project Development	Glasgow Development Agency
Mr Jim Robinson	Profit by Placement	Glasgow Development Agency
Mr Sean Mackney	CONTACT Consortium	Graduates for Greater Manchester
Ms Jo Cook	Group Resourcing and Development	Guinness plc
Ms Maggie Schofield	Student Services	King Alfreds University College Winchester
Ms Isabell Hodgson	School of Tourism and Hospitality	Leeds Metropolitan University
Mr Phil Margham	Head, Academic Development Unit	Liverpool John Moores University
Ms Maggon Paddon-Smith	Placements Enfield Campus	Middlesex University
Ms Elayne Burley	Director, Department of Employer Partnerships and Enterprise	Napier University
Ms Jennifer Graham	Department of Hospitality and Tourism Management	Napier University
Ms Melissa Highton	Department of Employer Partnerships and Enterprise	Napier University
Ms Sheila Lodge	School of Communications	Napier University
Mr Iain Marshall	Department of Psychology and Sociology	Napier University

Ms Lucy MacLeod	Department of Employer Partnerships and Enterprise	Napier University
Ms Sheila Stewart	Educational Development Unit	Napier University
Ms Jan Tunnock	Department of Hospitality and Tourism Management	Napier University
Ms Emma Frampton	Student Job Shop	Newcastle University
Ms Barbara Philips-Kerr	Placement Co-ordinator	Newcastle University
Ms Freda Tallintyer	Head of Regional Office	Northumbria University
Ms Kathy Mitchell	School of Hotel and Restaurant Management	Oxford Brookes University
Ms Candy Morley	School of Hotel and Restaurant Management	Oxford Brookes University
Mr David Wickenden	Management and Business Development	Profit Through People
Mr Paul Steer	NVQ Team Leader	RSA
Ms Amanda Wood	Work Experience Co-ordinator	Skills Exchange UMIST
Ms Amanda Brown	SIS Manager	Student Industrial Society
Mr David Rochester	HE/FE Advisor	Tyneside TEC
Mr John Bennett	Placements Co-ordinator	University College of Ripon and York St John
Mr David Browne	Film, TV, Literature and Theatre Studies	University College of Ripon and York St John
Ms Imogen Connolly	Recent graduate BA Hons Drama, Film and TV	University College of Ripon and York St John
Ms Sheila Cross	Careers Service	University College of Ripon and York St John
Mr Andy Hutchings	Business and Management Studies	University College of Ripon and York St John
Mr Tom Spencer	Performance Studies	University College of Ripon and York St John
Mr Geoff Stoakes	Faculty of Humanites	University College of Ripon and York St John
Ms Deborah Williams	Quality and Academic Staff Development	University College of Ripon and York St John
Mr Robert Pemble	School of Management	University of Abertay Dundee
Mr David Boyd	Faculty of the Built Environment	University of Central England
Mr Peter Ireland	Careers Department	University of Central England
Prof Howard Jackson	School of English	University of Central England
Ms Diane Kemp	Media and Communications	University of Central England
Ms Sue Thorn	Business School	University of Central England
Prof Phil Walkling	Directorate	University of Central England

Mr David Bagley	Career Development Unit	University of Central Lancashire
Prof Barry Lee	Dean of Computer Studies and Maths	University of Huddersfield
Ms Frances Ledgard	Business Liaison Officer (CRISP)	University of Leeds
Ms Maggie Challis	Learning and Teaching Institute	University of Nottingham
Ms Gill Crosby	Bristol Business School	University of the West of England
Mr George Stone	Bristol Business School	University of the West of England
Mr David Cox	Student Sponsorship Careers Advisory Service	University of Warwick
Prof Colin Appleby	Wolverhampton Corporate Enterprise Unit	University of Wolverhampton
Mr Doug Cauldwell	Academic Expansion Department	Worcester College of HE
Mr Roger Potter	Director	Youth for Britain

Written feedback

The following people provided researchers at the Centre for Research into Quality with written feedback and other material as part of the research. This list excludes members of the Steering Committee who provided invaluable input to the research (see Acknowledgements).

Mr Bob Mercer	University Centre for Accreditation and Negotiated Awards	Anglia Polytechnic University
Mr Philip Horn	Graduate Resourcing Dept	ASDA
Mr Bruce Davies	C and AC Department	Aston University
Dr Jackie Willis	School of Natural and Environmental Sciences	Coventry University
Ms Valerie Sewell	School of Engineering and Manufacture	De Montfort University
Mr Michael Howkins	Department of Mathematical Sciences	De Montfort University
Mr Simon Hamm	Careers and Placements Office	European Business School
Prof Oliver Fulton	Centre for the Study of Education and Training	Lancaster University
Dr Philip Frame	The Middlesex Business School	Middlesex University
Mr Stephen McNair	Associate Director	NIACE
Mr Colin Yarwood	Department of Surveying	Nottingham Trent University
Mr Ron Scott	Hospitality and Tourism Management	Queen Margaret College
Ms Shirley Earl	Educational Development Unit	Robert Gordon University
Mr Ian Paterson	Faculty of Management	Robert Gordon University
Mr John Berkeley OBE	Education and Careers	Rover Group
Ms Katie Hutton	Skills Development Directorate	Scottish Enterprise
Mr Nick Isherwood	Computing and IT	South Bank University

Mr Tom Calendair	Engineering Faculty	Strathclyde University
Ms Alison Lomax	Corporate Resourcing	Tesco
Ms Susanne Baker	Tourism, Hospitality and Leisure	Thames Valley University
Mr Mike Calvert	Centre for Careers and Academic Practice	The University of Liverpool
Ms Barbara Graham	Careers Service	University of Strathclyde
Ms Wendy Cringle	School of Management	University of Abertay Dundee
Ms Sheila Galloway	AGCAS Student Employment Services	University of Brighton
Mr Colin Davison	Local Examinations Syndicate	University of Cambridge
Dr John Wilson	Department of Business and Information Mangement	University of Central Lancashire
Mr Nick Ellis	Business School	University of Derby
Ms Barbara Littlewood	Department of Sociology	University of Glasgow
Dr Douglas MacGregor	Department of Physics and Astronomy	University of Glasgow
Mr Ian Burke	School of Business and Management	University of Greenwich
Dr L Banford	Divison of Chemistry	University of Hertfordshire
Ms L Dawson	Faculty of Natural Sciences	University of Hertfordshire
Ms Julie Wilkinson	MaPPiT School of Computing and Information Technology	University of Huddersfield
Mrs Val Butcher	Careers Service	University of Leeds
Mr Paul Jackson	Careers Service	University of Leeds
Ms Liane Langdon	Leeds University Union	University of Leeds
Dr Margaret Orchard	Staff and Departmental Development Unit	University of Leeds
Dr Peter Hawkins	Graduates into Employment Unit	University of Liverpool
Ms Janine Dodd	Enterprise Unit	University of Luton
Ms Jane Standley	Careers Advisory Service	University of Reading
Ms Kate Thornhill	School of Computing and Information Systems	University of Sunderland
Ms Dierdre Deery	Careers Service	University of Ulster
Ms Sandra Jennings	Computing and IT	University of Wolverhampton

Researchers at the Centre for Research into Quality are also grateful for the contributions by delegates at a number of conferences in 1997 where the research was discussed.